Preserving New England

PRESERVING
New England

Connecticut, Rhode Island, Massachusetts, Vermont, New Hampshire, Maine

JANE HOLTZ KAY
with PAULINE CHASE-HARRELL

Foreword by DAVID GILLESPIE
National Trust for Historic Preservation

PANTHEON BOOKS   New York

Library of Congress Cataloging in Publication Data

Kay, Jane Holtz.
  Preserving New England.

  1. Historic sites—New England—Conservation and
restoration. 2. Architecture—New England—Conservation
and restoration. 3. Landscape architecture—New
England—Conservation and restoration. I. Harrell,
Pauline Chase. II. Title.
F5.K39 1986   974   85-25980
ISBN 0-394-52037-8
ISBN 0-394-74395-4

Book design by Jennifer Dossin

Silhouette art by David Marshall

Manufactured in the United States of America

First Edition

CONTENTS

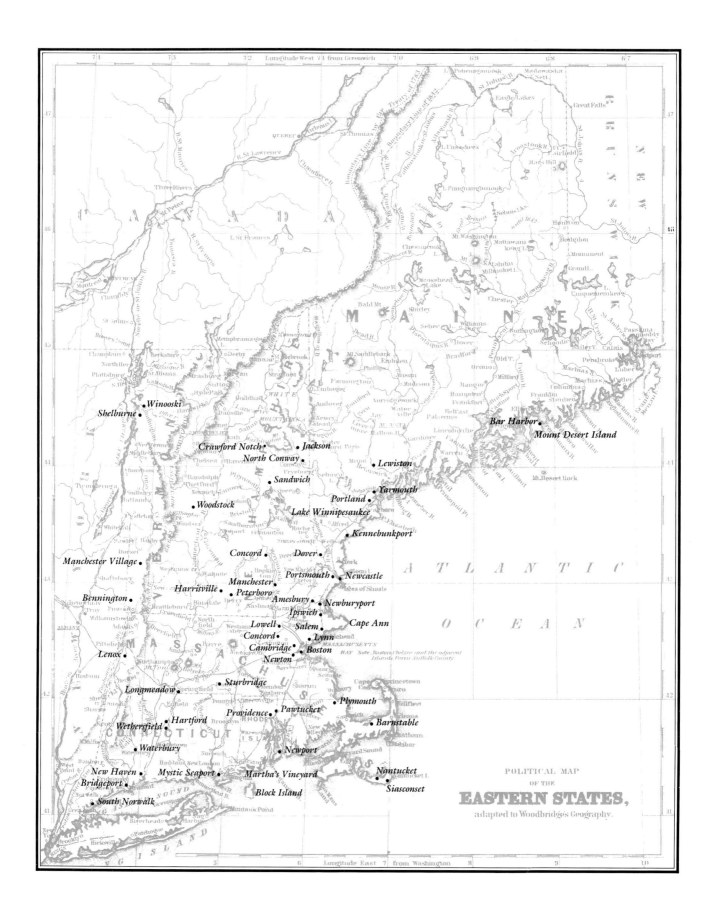

POLITICAL MAP
OF THE
EASTERN STATES,
adapted to Woodbridge's Geography.

Foreword

What is New England? The image that comes to mind is of tourist brochures. Of wiry New England farmers speaking in strange cadences. Of tiny Vermont communities where the chief industry is maple syrup and the denizens arrive at the white country church in sleighs. The idyllic New England is there if you look for it. But even in rural communities, you are likely to find more businessmen than farmers. Depending on your perspective, New England today is a land of high-tech manufacturing, ski resorts, downtown malls, and suburban communities. The urge to reconcile these competing themes is the raison d'être of the preservation movement in New England and the focus of *Preserving New England.*

A scant fifty miles from the Canadian border, newcomers and natives of Stannard, Vermont, are gradually restoring this splendid Gothic church silhouetted against the stark landscape of northern New England.

Change in New England has not gone unnoticed. In the eighteenth century, its citizens mourned the destruction of the countryside as virgin forests were cleared for settlers' farms. In the nineteenth century, Ralph Waldo Emerson blamed the railroad for bringing real-estate developers who looked at farms and thought, "I will plant a dozen houses on this pasture next moon and a village anon." Today we look back at the urban-renewal programs of the fifties and sixties with much the same horror, and beyond that a feeling that somehow much of what should have been New England has been lost to us forever.

The central question posed by this book is also the central question for all New Englanders: What do we preserve, and for whom? For many years, efforts at preservation were individualistic, concentrating on single buildings, on small pieces of the whole. Those efforts raised the consciousness of many in this country and are still emulated. But preservation in that context was regarded simply as a backdrop against which change occurred. Change itself was equated with progress.

Not so now. Today, preservation is popular in New England, and change another matter. Experiments in preservation abound, as *Preserving New England* demonstrates, and billions of dollars pour into preservation activities. The movement has gone beyond singling out lone buildings and marshaling forces to save them. Preservationists seek to establish the tools to insure that preservation remains an active force in communities everywhere.

When the National Trust established a Northeast Regional Office in Boston in 1972, there were fewer than eighty preservation organizations in the region. Today there are more than six hundred groups of activists and several hundred historic-district commissions. State historic-preservation offices have made vast progress in completing the surveys of historic buildings mandated under the Preservation Act of 1966. Preservationists lobby their legislatures as well as the national Congress, gaining the political clout that translates into grant programs, environmental-protection legislation, and perhaps most important of all, special tax treatment for preservation activity. Smaller communities across the region are revitalizing their centers using innovative programs like the National Trust's Main Street approach to downtown revitalization, described here. Major urban areas are seeking ways to channel new development, and the reader will note that even in hot real-estate markets like Boston, the city's new "design for downtown" guidelines aim to insure that we have both a modern city and a city that respects its past. All this is well documented in *Preserving New England.*

It is clear, then, that we in preservation have established our right to have a say in the future of our communities. But what are we saying? With the right to define our destiny comes the obligation to move forward and develop new programs, new tools, and new ways to secure it. Like all movements, we have had our successes and failures—and, lest anyone forget, major historic structures are still coming down all around us. National Historic Landmarks such as the Trinity Church in Newport are in imminent danger of collapse. In recent years, fires have destroyed major mill buildings in Fall River and whole sections of cities, containing much of their historic fabric. Highway projects continue to threaten the historic landscape, and farms continue to fall victim to abandonment or second-home development. This, too, comprises part of the picture shown in *Preserving New England.*

The list of successes chronicled in this invaluable book shows just how popular preservation has become here. But the threat it reveals is equally clear and compelling. Freud in the 1930s admitted his puzzlement with the tendency of men to hold on to the past. "How has it come about that so many people have adopted this strange attitude of hostility to progress?" he asked. Amazingly, some still ask that question. We have not yet changed the mind-set that equates "progress" with the changes we wreak on the landscape. This book challenges the reader to confront that attitude and to help create an atmosphere in which preservation and "progress" are linked. Then we will have the answer to the central question, "What do we preserve, and for whom?"

DAVID GILLESPIE
Regional Director, Northeast Regional Office
National Trust for Historic Preservation

Acknowledgments

"This car climbed Mt. Washington," reads the bumper sticker. As my own car bumper-to-bumpered along the miseries of Route 1 in southern Maine, traced the crowded curves of the rural landscape of Vermont, or slithered into the last parking space in Boston's Leather District, it seemed an apt slogan for the odyssey. The journey to gain a lofty perspective followed paved routes, on and off the beaten path.

Above all, this four-year journey across New England's 66,000 square miles was powered by the vision of the National Trust for Historic Preservation. In 1980, the trust conceived a series of books to chart what may be the major movement of our day: the urge to preserve and protect the built environment. The trust's decision could not have been more timely. A search for place and identity characterizes a nation in the throes of change,

Entrance of Italianate house in Grafton, Massachusetts.

and is played out poignantly in this time-marked corner of the country.

My thanks also goes to the National Endowment for the Arts. Its Design Arts Fellowship provided both financial assistance and a sign of approval from a field more given to lauding three-dimensional works than to supporting such literary labors.

Narrowing New England down to a handful of case studies was enough to make any author wish she were "perfectly ambidexter" (as a contemporary said of Cotton Mather's two-faced statements at the Salem witch trials). Here, too, help was needed. And help was at hand from a vast and diverse array of advisors, friends, readers, and colleagues. Their endless generosity and their plural points of view of both the built and natural environments contributed to a holistic sense of the region. Gratitude of the most heartfelt sort can be rendered only alphabetically, then, to these among them: Richard Candee, John Coolidge, Abbott Lowell Cummings, Stephen Fox, David Hall, William Hart, Ken Hoffman, Charles Hosmer, Chester Liebs, Keith Morgan, Bruce MacDougall, Marcia Myers, Susan Park, Robert Rettig, and Wesley Ward. Robert Severy, again at the author's right hand, maintained his matchless vigil in pursuit of accuracy.

In addition, a thank-you note remains on permanent deposit for the assembled crew of 102 South Street, chief among them Dorothea Hass. Their keen appreciation of the subject was paralleled only by their friendship and support.

Preserving New England relies on its photographs, and credit for the bulk of these goes to Frederica Matera. Thanks are due not only for her abundant photographic talents but for her share in the editing and critiquing; her sensitivity to the environment made her an ideal companion as well as photographer, and the mileage we clocked is only one measure of that contribution. Care beyond mere picture-taking also characterizes the evocative portraits of the past by Randolph Langenbach and the strong documentations by Steve Rosenthal and the seventy other photographers and institutions whose contributions are visible here. The visual records of the region were precious and essential, whether in the SPNEA archives, ably shepherded by librarian Elinor Reichlin; in the Library of Congress with its FSA photographs; or in the many regional repositories. Each has added the same historic depth to this undertaking as the architecture adds to the landscape.

The record-holder for endurance, good nature, and acute commentary remains the book's editor, Betsy Amster, who managed a rare mix of firmness and generosity in contouring this text and photographs. For welding the words and pictures into a graceful volume, praise is due to designer Jennifer

Dossin. Thanks for the nitty-gritty of turning a manuscript into a book go to typists Argie Staples, Vykki Dewsnap, and Jill Sakardy.

This book is not only a witness to the labor of preservationists, family, and friends, however. It is a testament to the hopes for the next generation. As such, it is dedicated with love and admiration to my daughters Jacqueline and Julie. May the New England they and countless others create be a worthy successor to the one they have inherited.

Jane Holtz Kay

This book has indeed been an odyssey, through the New England mind as well as the New England states. I have long sensed, as I attended conferences and workshops of the National Trust and the National Alliance of Preservation Commission in other parts of the country, that preservation was somehow different here: if not necessarily more successful, at least more integrated into everyday life. The history of our built environment and the origins of the movement to preserve it hold the clues to this difference. Delving into that history anew with the focus of this book brought a new understanding of our professional roots; discussions with colleagues throughout the region and across the country deepened that understanding.

To the many colleagues and friends who contributed to this book, I would like to echo the above thanks. In addition I would like to express my gratitude to the many generations of "little old ladies (and men) in tennis shoes" who have struggled before us to preserve New England. Without them, there would be precious little for this generation to preserve, and we would have had precious little to write about.

Pauline Chase-Harrell

Preserving New England

Winding road and leaf-strewn lawn in Marlboro,
Vermont.

Prologue

Banishing the Myth

*N*ew England is the American backdrop: everybody's hometown, the nation's Christmas card, summer vacation, history, idyll. *Here is the church* (white). *Here is the steeple* (white). *Open the doors and see all the people* (Puritan people, of course). Yankees, stern but caring, they are tending to their God within and, with equal rigor, grooming their landscape without. Their center is the eternal village green, attended by another constant, the spired church; and beyond that their farms and red barns settle into their rolling hills. The operative word here is *nestled.* The operative attitude? Protective. Who would change a blade of this mythic New England?

Banishing the Myth

The view from the distinctly New England window where this book began is of an excavation hole that has spread as fast as the first New England settlements. Daily, a giant-clawed derrick flicks its wrists and, like a dinosaur pawing an anthill, shifts the landscape. Outside the same window, a mini-park holds benches and a bronze fountain. At the center of the fountain, a turn-of-the-century cupid dances in the sun. On its edges, two less upright twentieth-century "symbols" sleep in the sun. The park benches are their New England.

"You'll see a humongous Sheraton," says a guide to our trip through the six-state region. "Take a right."

"There's a ghastly King's Mall," says another, offering directions. "Exit there."

The mall, the chain, the franchise: these are the landmarks of their New England—Maine, New Hampshire, Vermont, Massachusetts, Rhode Island, Connecticut, 1980s style.

"It's a little yellow house next to the big tin trailer," still another friend describes her vacation home. "That's New Hampshire."

Many talk of their New England with poetry: all russets and crimsons, the oranges and yellows of autumn. The color coders of New England even offer their views in scientific terms: "70 percent color," one newspaper terms the foliage, "80 percent," "40 percent." Percent of green leaf? Percent of ultimate tones? What does it mean? Who decided to rate the leaves this way anyhow? Did they put them through a computer?

"How to look at the leaves," the Vermont Travel Division tells you: "Drive toward the sunlight. Get off the highways."

Who, for that matter, can see the leaves for the automobiles? The bands of tourists must go out in scouting parties of two—a passenger to observe the color, and a driver to keep eyes on the fenders of the cars as they chain north. Booking into the classic

The underside of New England: semi trailers in Tiverton, Rhode Island, and tanks in Chelsea, Massachusetts.

white inns or bedding down in motels, the foliage fans alternate the seasonal colors with the electronic tints of the TV screen.

That, of course, is our New England, too.

Certainly, our ancestors had a cleaner, lovelier sense of their New England. The nineteenth century literally collected vistas: they commissioned them from artists, kept them for decades. Poised on some hill, these artists surveyed the sweep of a place. Their images might show the proverbial city beside the water where the water wheels turned, a center or village core, greenery all around, clutches of houses, farms fanning out, some livestock, and perhaps a picturesque couple scanning the scene.

Who can say if harmony, depicted by the scene painter or lithographer, was really there or if he imposed it for the sake of art and flattery? However shaped, the scene said something about the commonality of outlook—the clear sense of identity in this older New England. From his lofty perch, the view-maker conveyed a shared and idealized vision; it was the embodiment of a consensus and way of life manifest in the design for human activity upon the land.

Today's twelve-million-plus New Englanders share no such harmonious vistas. Where can they climb even to pretend to look for them? The highways that curl or circle the region's cities and towns offer today's perspective, and it is a discordant one. The vista-seeker looking toward the capital of New Hampshire from Route 93, for instance, must look past the orange roof of a Howard Johnson's to sight the golden dome of Concord's State House. Travel by Providence along I-95 for a vista, and you see oil tanks hugging the landscape, a papier-mâché bug squatting atop a pest control plant. In Hartford, Route 86 offers the motorist no overview at all, only a plunge through a tunnel, structures to either side. Enter Boston, Portland, or any place via an interstate, then, and there is no ruling order or viewpoint, simply the random hand of the twentieth century,

Quintessential New England highway architecture: the Blair Road Bridge in Campton, New Hampshire.

with neither a shared ethic of the land nor the set of rules to create one. What Wendell Berry might call the "unsettlers of America" have ravaged the region. Their work accosts the traveler's eye.

The walker, too, finds a disparate, if more often agreeable, array of landscapes. The remains of the past are real and wonderful, but by and large, the passerby finds that the built artifacts of our generation clutter the surface of New England. The new look, ruled by the dictates of the most mindless kind of commerce, jars the landscape. A "Viking Cadillac" sign on the outskirts of Newport says no more about that town's heritage than "Witch City" labels on Salem's fast-food stands or Deer Crossing condominiums on Cape Cod. The nastiness, the sameness of the twentieth-century product looks shoddier still against the legacy of a land whose contours show three and a half centuries of settlement.

The Shape of the Land

To understand those contours one must look at New England in terms of an even older heritage, the

A unity of town and country: Concord, New Hampshire, as depicted by a nineteenth-century viewmaker.

heritage of the Ice Ages. New England's topography records the shifting ice flows of a glacial era that subsided only ten thousand years ago—an instant in the half-billion years during which nature has subdued and shaped the land.

The region's ancient mountains, high as any in Europe during their glory days, rose with the great upheavals of the earth's crust that ended 150 million years ago. Sweeping across the northeast portion of the continent, the sheets of ice scooped out the valleys and defined them with waves of pebbles and boulders; they carved glacial potholes, deep grooves for ponds, and rolling hills. The human flow redefined the work of nature: first, the Indians with their fires that cleared the forests, their simple agricultural villages, and their trails or trading paths that shaped the future highways; then the Europeans with their settlements cutting ever-deeper wedges inland from the coast. By 1840, farmers and townspeople had marked the landscape as visibly as the force of nature itself, clearing three-quarters of the forest land for agriculture. That, too, was transitory. Today, only one out of three New England acres shows the signs of plow or builder. Two out of three again wear a cover of woods.

Thus, what passes for natural environment is, in fact, one reshaped over time by human hands—the pattern of farm and city traced on a stubborn and pronounced terrain.

Geography as Destiny

It is easier to describe New England's landscape in poetry or metaphor than with facts or maps. What Thoreau called "the bared and bended arm of Massachusetts . . . boxing with Northeast storms" still gives us the sense of Cape Cod's outline and spirit. Few straight lines limn New England's six-thousand-mile coastline. Its crooked edge of bays and inlets makes the word *erratic* an understatement.

Ruggedness characterizes the terrain as a whole: the dominant peaks of the White Mountains to the north, the Green Mountains to the west, the Taconic range to the south, and the hilly farmlands. Few surfaces of New England suffer the tedium, or for that matter, the ease, of flatness. Seldom does New England see the fertile flood plains of the South or the level farmlands of the Midwest. Rough edges score

The twentieth century swept its automania across New England. Here, the view from Charlestown's City Square.

the coastline so severely that the peninsulas between Boothbay and Calais, Maine (four hundred of them in a scant two hundred miles by one count) outnumber the towns. Even New Hampshire's scant twelve-mile coastline of marshy inlets by the Piscataqua and the Merrimack rivers meanders crookedly from border to border. Stretch out this curving coastline from Lubec on the northern seacoast of Maine to Greenwich, Connecticut, and you could frame the continent.

Water adds to the irregularity. It is New England's major motif. "The land is loved by ocean," wrote Amos R. Wells in his poem "The Garden of New England,"

> *far and deep*
> *The long bays reach among the sloping fields,*
> *And tenderly the shining waters creep*
> *Where waiting marsh a silent welcome yields*
> *And slow brown currents in the shadows run,*
> *And thick-ranked sedges glitter in the sun.*

No other region has the range of wet places: water from massive inland bodies (Lake Champlain, Lake Winnipesaukee, Moosehead Lake), slivers of sea, slim inlets, and porcelain ponds. Brackish waters stand slack, dense with seaweed among Cape Ann's boulders; and dark bays lap at pilings in Westport, Maine. Water races, crashes, oozes. That water has made all the difference in the tale to be told.

Forest covers most of the region and tells New England's story too. New Hampshire's second growth of scruffy pines says that the land is no longer worth the care of farming or husbandry, while Northern Maine survives, if barely, on the commerce of woods seeded like orchards. Elsewhere, Vermont farmers have tugged out saplings to maintain their rolling fields for agriculture, and only a few trees punctuate the view. Thoreau saw this diversity more than a century ago: "Some rotten trunk, which in

Water all around: the Mad River mists the air and twists from placid to frothy in Moretown, Vermont.

Maine cumbers the ground, and is, perchance, thrown into the water on purpose, is here [Cape Cod] thus carefully picked up, split, and dried and husbanded." His New England is our New England, too.

Many Times, Many Climates

Beyond the sense of place, New England has the sense of time—time measured in a span older than most in this country of the new. Like Troy, this region contains evidence of successive sackings, as Tracy Kidder observed in *The Soul of a New Machine.* The deserted trackless beds of railroads and the cellar holes and crumbling stone walls of textile mills leave traces barely visible among the condominiums and malls, the highways and highrises.

There is a feel, too, of many climates. "And they that know the winters of that country know them to be sharp and violent, and subject to cruel and fierce storms," William Bradford wrote three centuries ago. The seasons declare their singularity and define the landscape further, bringing us the sands of winter skirred by snow and the raucous summer shore "which makes flashing answer to the sun," described three centuries later in naturalist Henry Beston's *The Outermost House.* The pink dogwood of spring and the darkened bark of winter, the blue seas of late spring and the fine gray stillness of autumn engage the senses.

Henry Adams saw such shifts as the soul of the region. "The chief charm of New England was harshness of contrasts and extremes of sensibility—a cold that froze the blood, and a heat that boiled it," he wrote of his nineteenth-century childhood in *The Education of Henry Adams:* "Winter and summer, cold and heat, town and country, force and freedom, marked two modes of life and thought, balanced like

The architecture of work: a brooding New England barn and New London's strong stone lighthouse.

lobes of the brain. Town was winter confinement . . . country, only seven miles away, was liberty, diversity, outlawry."

An Architecture of Contrasts

New England architecture, like its seasons, displays the full spectrum of colors: Main Street façades of rosy brick and yellow Maine farms; white churches dappled by sunlight and gingerbread Victorians edged in russet, orange, and brown. And the full range of shapes: the sweeping roofs and subtly sculpted façades of Newport's Shingle-Style mansions; the lofty Belvedere of a Portsmouth captain's mansion; the brooding planes of a brick mill rising above a canal in Holyoke; and, in the *nouvelle* New England, the peaked skylights of Sugarbush condominiums.

Like its topography—at times a loping landscape, at times a stark silhouette—New England's architecture sometimes conforms to, sometimes contradicts, its surroundings. In Vermont, silos stand at right angles to the rolling fields, while a clutch of barns hugs the horizon. At times, it is retiring (the clapboard houses and barns huddling in the New Hampshire mountains); at times, assertive (row upon row of sun-struck windows proclaiming at once the size of a mill and the regimentation inside); and, on occasion, it is surreal (a giant power transformer become an eerie ghost in a western Massachusetts snowstorm).

It is an architecture of diversity in style and size and magnificence, from the mansions of Newport's Cliff Walk to the cluster of tiny cottages on Nantucket's Sciasconset side, from the workaday three-deckers of Hartford, Worcester, Cambridge, Bangor to the delights of Victorian gingerbread at Oak Bluffs, Martha's Vineyard. The diversity is paralleled in complete cities: granite and red-brick Boston;

New England's countless colleges define the mind-set and the landscape. Here, Yale in New Haven.

slick, glassy-eyed Hartford; delicate old white-clapboard Portsmouth and Newburyport; the dark russet mill town of Lewiston, Maine.

The greenery that laces the built landscape shares the variety. A simple ribbon of grass fronts the houses along Longmeadow, Massachusetts, or Litchfield, Connecticut. Statues measure the blocks along the stately promenade of Boston's Commonwealth Avenue. A broad promenade overlooks Portland's harbor. The classic New England common that centers endless towns contrasts with the naturalistic nineteenth-century parks curving picturesquely at their edges.

The Life of the Landscape

New England's vital statistics measure the diversity of its life today. We could tally New England in miles of electric power lines or stone walls, in gallons of maple syrup exported or barrels of oil imported, in cases of silicon chips produced or acres of old looms lying idle. We could enumerate its colleges and universities with their eight hundred thousand students,

from the urban mega-scholarship of Harvard, MIT, or Boston University, to the College of the Atlantic in Bar Harbor, where a few hundred students live out an L. L. Bean lifestyle, to bustling state universities where century-old "aggie" schools sit side by side with computer labs.

We could scan its demographics: almost thirteen million people live in the six states, half within eighty miles of Boston. Here, at the upper end of the "Bos-Wash" megalopolis, southern New Englanders jostle on some of the nation's most densely populated urban turf, while their northern peers may live in Maine's unincorporated land.

If New England was once defined by its literary elite of the "Concord Renaissance," today's lifestyles show in its newsstand literature. It is *Country Journal* with its reverence for uncomplicated ways of life, and the *Atlantic Monthly,* attuned to New England–bred literacy; it is the liberal *Boston Globe,* the reactionary *Manchester Union Leader,* the gingham-curtain *Yankee Magazine,* and the of-the-minute *New England Monthly.* Their diverse pages reflect the diverse politics of this land of the town meeting where everyone takes part—and fiercely. Be it New Hampshire where license plates proclaim "Live Free or Die," or Cambridge, which fights for a nuclear-free zone, politics is an intense affair.

New England's people match the land for quirky individuality. In a nation of back-to-back Burger-villes and TV-cloned accents, "Yankee" still has a meaning all its own. That meaning—the "true" Yankee—is as elusive as the region's varied building forms. To an outsider, a Yankee is an inhabitant of New England's six states, whether a flinty Vermonter or a feisty Boston Irish politician. To an urban New Englander, it is a rural farmer living his life to the pace of the Yankee twang; to the immigrant, or grandchild of immigrants, it is a member of the small enclave of Brahmin heirs living in Boston's Back Bay

An abandoned house just north of Camden, Maine. The poverty that plagues New England is not always picturesque.

or Beacon Hill. But, however interpreted, the word defines our New England.

A Common Landscape

For all its plurality, then, there is a commonality. Individuality is New England's state of mind. The region's very identity still allows—cannot do other than allow—its differences. Character is a virtue encouraged here, in people as in landscapes: strong temperaments, strong building styles parallel the distinctiveness of time and place, of climate and geography. "We know, perhaps, better than others, the implacability of life," novelist Robert Parker wrote. "In the effulgence of July, we do not forget January. This is the moral condition of New England, the alternate contracting and relaxation of our spiritual frame has made us sinewy (and stiff, perhaps). We know that death is the mother of beauty, and we have stood beside the frozen water and shivered in the wind." Shivering in the wind, taking in the full measure of sunlight, the New Englander indeed has a code that has given character to our New England.

> *Use it up*
> *Wear it out*
> *Make it do*
> *Or do without*

It is doggerel, but also our ultimate ethic, an adage from New England's past that has become an environmental imperative not only for these six states and for those conscious of their heritage but for a nation concerned with survival in an energy-short, resource-scarce future. New England is a mature region whose capacity to husband its resources and preserve and enhance its riches could—in fact, should—become a model for the nation.

Sometimes it does not seem so. The water war is on. Or is it the land war? Or the highway war? Or the resources war? Whichever, it is raging across the New England landscape. New England suffers from underdevelopment, some say. The stately old homes of Maine crumble from lack of life, and the woods inch across their acreage. New England is plagued by overdevelopment, others demonstrate. Corporate-image towers and the gaping maws of parking garages dehumanize Fairfield County's cities; high-tech plants eat up the countryside.

Needs and pressures vary. Lovers of the vanishing loon pray for rain (not acid) to keep tourists away from their Lake Winnipesaukee refuge; motel operators hope for endless sunshine. Some labor to preserve New England's farmland and rural ways; others take on the guardianship of city life. Those who, like Henry James, Sr., find bricks and mortar much "more succulent pasturing than the rocks that still stand" alternate with those who look askance at the seething cities. The new gentry flock to our towns while their drop-out peers flee from them. Conservationists tend to the green landscape, preservationists to the harder edges of buildings, often mindless of the overlapping need for both.

Prosperity transforms the Hancock School in Lexington, Massachusetts, into condominiums. Hard times keep a school empty in Lisbon, Maine.

Can we have it all? Can we have everything that old New England offered—zesty urban life and quiet country places? Historian J. B. Jackson once wrote that he liked New England best when it was "serious and poor." Who with a caring eye for the environment would not choose the aesthetics of rural poverty over the boisterous boutiquism of a mallified Main Street or commercial strip? Those mired in the poverty, of course. For them, the malls and developments represent access to the mainstream of American life. They want to trade weathered clapboards, worn linoleum, and leaky plumbing for the glossy comforts of vinyl siding and waxless Congoleum. Character in New England should not be a synonym for decay and deprivation. Preservation should not mean stifling change.

Change defined and defines the landscape of New England and a living world. Change could be, as the Transcendentalists believed it, joining a nature ever in flux. But change, twentieth-century style, has come to mean a corruption of all that makes the region worthwhile: the change from a graceful landscape to wall-to-wall chain stores, the change from comfortable corner stores to a griddle of sizzling fast food franchises. The gap between a hands-on grasp of nature and a high-tech scorn of it widens. Can it be reversed? Can the completeness, the diversity that is New England, be saved? Can we enrich hard-pressed lives, yet "make it do"?

Our New England ancestors left us a gift, a landscape of urban and rural life in a tenuous balance; they preserved New England. Can we do the same for the next century? That is our hope and our ideal. We want New England to endure and yet to change. Above all, we want it to respect its identity, as it always has. This is what *Preserving New England* is all about.

PART ONE
History

Plymouth as reconstructed at Plimoth Plantation.

1. The Building of New England

With the certainty of the seasons and the constancy of the centuries, New England has bowed to the myth of Thanksgiving. In annual, sometimes it seems eternal, celebration of both fact and fable, school children have traced the gray legion of Pilgrim fathers and mothers, the plump "Pilgrim" turkeys, the solid "Pilgrim" log cabins. Carrying myth into adulthood, poets, painters, sculptors, and pageant directors have recreated the first footfall on the "stern and rockbound coast" and the first Thanksgiving feast. Worshippers of this perfected past have raised, lowered, moved, encased, engraved, sketched,

Plymouth Rock was honored with a portico designed by Hammatt Billings in 1889, shown here. In 1920, New Englanders replaced it with the "up-to-date" monument that stands today.

and hymned Plymouth Rock. Cast in the romantic chiaroscuro of Nathaniel Hawthorne, myth obscures the founding of New England. Reality recedes. Can we ever retrieve the true events?

Fortunately, sources survive, for few historical happenings have had the scribes and documents of

the settlement of New England. The Pilgrims and the Puritans and, for that matter, the entrepreneurs who undertook the settlement of Maine and New Hampshire left copious records. To retrieve these sources and discard the intervening layers of myth would tell only half the story, however. The myths themselves hold hints of New England's character. In fact, they too shaped it.

From the beginning, New Englanders knew that they had set upon an historic course. Aware of that destiny, the self-conscious settlers saw the founding of New England as a text for posterity; they must record every detail for their heirs. Soon, however, historical consciousness went beyond mere notation. It took on a quality of reverence for the past. Early on, New Englanders looked back to halcyon days: the God-fearing days of the uncompromising Puritans in one century and the palmy days of China clippers in another, rural innocence and the pastoral common in one era, humming spindles and restless textile mills in another. Nostalgia and myth infused the recollecting.

In homage to these bygone glories, New Englanders have catalogued and annotated their archives and cherished their Rose Medallion china. They have embedded obelisks and planted trees to "restore" their mythic commons, turned fishermen's shanties into vacation homes and outdated mills into housing for the elderly. Even when building anew, they have embraced or invoked the past, adapting the sweep of seventeenth-century saltbox shapes to nineteenth-century vacation "cottages," sheathing real estate offices in weathered shingles, plastering Federal porticos on modern supermarkets.

The past was, and is, so much with the New England. Little matter which past and which present. Each generation interprets those distant days anew and builds accordingly, adding yet another layer of landscape to those of its ancestors.

The Settlement of New England in Fact

We can narrate the story of the first of these ancestors straightforwardly. In 1620, the small band of separatists known to history as the Pilgrims planted the first successful colony in New England at the place they named Plymouth. Yet, it was their neighbors to the north, the Puritans, who eventually absorbed them. John Winthrop's followers had greater advantages from the start and greater influence in the end. From the settlement of Massachusetts Bay Colony in 1630, the Puritan leader and his followers set many of New England's indelible patterns. It was here that the Puritans turned their theories of a perfect society into real, if imperfect, communities.

Boston, with its three hills and ample harbor, became the center of that colony and remained the hub of the region's universe. The Bay Colony that surrounded it grew faster than any other. By 1643, Massachusetts held more settlers than all the rest of English America: two dozen towns with over fifteen thousand settlers. From here, the ideas and institutions of Puritan New England went forth.

Center it might be, but not everyone found a Heavenly City in John Winthrop's New Jerusalem. Individuals with their own views of God's word founded other Promised Lands in the ample geography of New England. Thomas Hooker was such an individualist. Disgruntled with religious life in the Bay Colony, he took several congregations with him. Others followed, and by 1636 they had founded four new towns in the Connecticut Valley. Theophilus Eaton and John Davenport headed further south two years later, establishing the New Haven colony on the Connecticut coast. By 1662, England had incorporated both areas into the single colony of Connecticut.

Another charismatic malcontent, the young minister Roger Williams, carried his principles of separation of church and state and absolute freedom of conscience to start Rhode Island at Providence in 1636. Anne Hutchinson, also banished from Massachusetts for her teachings, settled in Newport. Other dissenting communities soon joined the exodus, coalescing in the colony of Rhode Island.

In the north, colonization came more slowly, and its inspiration was less spiritual. Captain John Mason and Sir Fernando Gorges, landholders more concerned with their pocketbooks than with their eternal souls, squabbled over the land north of the Merrimack River, slowing settlement in Maine and New Hampshire. In 1623, they agreed to divide their lands along the Piscataqua River. In time, settlers filtered into the southern area and, in 1679, New Hampshire became a colony. Maine moved more slowly. Annexed to Massachusetts in 1691, it remained under the commonwealth's control until 1820. Vermont also dallied, mired in border disputes. Ethan Allen and his brothers did not make settlement secure in the Green Mountain state until the Revolution. Nonetheless, in ripples of discontent and diffusion, the map of New England enlarged quickly. Before the first century of settlement had elapsed, five regions of settlement under four colonial governments had spread across its boundaries. To this day, the landscape of New England testifies to the way those first settlers thought and felt.

Patterning the Land

Keenly aware of casting a new, and perfect, society, the Puritans laid strong foundations—social, governmental, and architectural—that were to be reflected in New England's built environment for centuries to come.

In their structured order, life was defined by covenants, agreements between man and God, and between man and man. Above all, the community mattered. When they called Massachusetts the "Commonwealth," they meant it: the common wellbeing. To serve the Commonwealth, the Puritans invented the most characteristic form of the New England landscape, the New England town. Drawing upon familiar English precedents, they combined the three organizational units of English life—the village, the parish, and the borough—into one geographic entity. Those who lived in the town participated economically, religiously, and politically; its form reflected their unified views.

At the core of the Puritan universe, and so at the center of the town, was the meetinghouse, which held religious and political meetings and, early on, housed the school as well. Intent on full participation, the early New Englanders decreed it on the landscape. They legislated a centralized community. Massachusetts law initially forbade constructing a house more than half a mile from the meetinghouse. The pull of free land at the edges of the town soon led to the law's breach and finally its repeal. The attitude lingered, nonetheless. The urge for a clus-

At work and at play, in summer and winter, New Englanders filled the common. Here, the common at Greenfield, Massachusetts. Originating in the Puritan concept of shared space, the meeting ground became a reigning feature of the region.

tered settlement shaped the development of New England in the profoundest way.

Common land—commonly owned, commonly used—distinguished the New England town. A "church green" stood at the center, but common lands of woodlots, pasturage, and, in waterside towns, "ways to the water" also embodied this sense of sharing in the landscape. The Puritan attitude toward use and management of these lands for the common weal also shaped New England.

The Puritan concept of stewardship, so central to their belief system, went beyond management of the common lands; it manifested itself in a total ethos. God's gifts were not to be squandered. This religious tenet suited the landscape of New England: the Puritans found a resistant soil which demanded good management. The spiritual belief also dovetailed with their desire for compact settlements.

The Puritan elevation of mind over matter made itself manifest in an aesthetic, even an ethic, of appearances, too. Aiming to avoid the semblance of vanity, they espoused an austerity that took root and

hallmarked the region. Not that the Puritans scorned beauty. Rather, they found more comfort in objects whose practicality justified their appeal. In days to come, Chippendale chairs, Adamesque drawing-rooms, even Victorian architecture, seen through New England eyes and retooled to New England taste, showed a reserve grounded in this Puritan suspicion of "vanity" and respect for functional restraint.

Old England in the New

In their architecture, the Puritans looked to a simpler heritage than that of the England they had left. A rural people, still imbued with the traditions of the Middle Ages, they rejected the Renaissance ideals

seeping into their homeland for the medieval ones recalled. The home they built in their New England belonged to this more distant past. A two-story, rectangular carcass of heavy oak timbers, it was fitted together with mortises and tenons visible inside. Whitewashed plaster covered the interior, and riven clapboards or shingles the exterior. The "jetty," or overhang of one story, marked by carved pendils or "drops" at the corners, still recalls the medieval heritage in a striking way.

The image of this early house remains engraved in the New England vision: there are the tiny windows with their small diamond panes, set in lead at regular intervals; the door, more or less centered; the steep, narrow stairway coiling upward before a massive central chimney; and the kitchen fireplace, so huge that it swallowed "cords of wood as a whale does boats," in Herman Melville's words. The lean-to attached to the back of the house for a "buttery," a summer kitchen, or a "borning room" gave the house its saltbox profile.

Time changed the house. More lean-tos, gables, and ells came jutting outward. These angled additions, meandering like wayward children from the center of the New England house, gave an individual stamp to the first and basic form. Both heir and progenitor, this yeoman farmhouse transported from eastern England set the course for architecture in New England.

If the saltbox house was a throwback to rural England, the New England meetinghouse was a native creation. It had to be, for nothing like the New England Puritan church existed in old England. Here, the Puritans were dominant; their meetinghouses could suit their own vision. That vision dictated a plain, square building, generally of two stories. "Forthright and severe, like the Puritan divines who preached within it," Samuel Eliot Morison described the Old Ship Church in Hingham, Massachusetts.

Straight wooden pews surrounded an austere pulpit set against the wall opposite the entrance. A gallery, added as the congregation grew, often lined the upper walls. However novel the concept of the meetinghouse, its construction and use for both church and town meetings harked back to the medieval folk tradition of its builders. It became the ancestor of generations of churches, schools, and town halls in New England. Its influence also traveled westward, where its descendants became the symbol of the architecture that says "America" across the continent.

The harsh New England climate, so unlike the temperate British Isles, dictated other changes. The New World's resources reinforced the shift. Colder winters and hotter summers decayed the traditional thatched roof: a fire hazard, it was soon outlawed. Stucco, characteristic of the "half-timbered" construction of England, also did not hold. Wooden clapboards or shingles, cut from the abundant forests of the New World, soon sheathed the buildings of the region. Before long, the colonists created a tradition of their own, seduced by the appeal of wood and discouraged by the damp chill of masonry.

Beset by nature, New Englanders accommodated their architecture to its demands. Center chimneys that countered the cold and retained heat became standard. Was it medieval aesthetics or the ability to shed snow that led to the steep saltbox roofs? Whichever, they functioned well and endured. Bitter winters also led to the careful siting of houses. The Jackson house in Portsmouth, New Hampshire, might have sat for a portrait of the "dear old parsonage" described by a New Hampshire woman writing a full two centuries later: "a tolerably large, dark, unpainted house, two stories in front, full of windows, to admit all the genial influences of the south, while on the north it sloped down so that one might lay his hand on the roof." From such beginnings, New England's "connected farmstead" would slowly evolve. House fixed to milkroom, milkroom to woodshed, on and on to barn, the living chain framed a sheltered yard in a deliberate—we now say "ecological"—response to the environment.

Setting and Survival

"Yankee ingenuity," as well as Yankee architecture, sprouted from New England's rocky earth. Farms then, as now, were small. Clearing his lot of trees, freeing the land of rocks, the farmer stacked stone and boulder along the edge. Thus the classic stone walls of New England were born. Trailing through field and forest today, they too are constants of the region.

On their small holdings, New England farm families tended to their own needs, amassing farmsteads of offshoot buildings surrounded by woodlots, pastures, and tilled fields. Here and there, towns grew up to serve the farmers, as much to satisfy old communal urges for schools and churches as to provide the economic sevices of gristmills and sawmills, taverns and stores.

Along the coast, the ocean trade dictated still another environment. As New Englanders turned to the sea to supplement the meager returns of the land, once again the economy of survival shaped their space. Fish and whales, trade and shipbuilding lured the ambitious to New England's ports. Before the Revolution, coastal towns swelled in the wake of the sea-borne enterprise of the ingenious Yankees. Waterside land in places like Boston, Salem, Portsmouth, and Newport grew dear and was subdivided. Narrow streets pushed through former house and garden lots. Sail lofts, chandleries, countinghouses, West India goods shops, and merchants' homes jammed the bustling lanes. The crowded wharves

Time itself seems to have tacked on the rambling additions that settle into the landscape around the seventeenth-century Fairbanks house in Dedham, Massachusetts.

Jostling for space, seaside towns like Plymouth narrowed the Georgian style into "half houses" and "three-quarter houses," as can be seen in this nineteenth-century view of closely built Leyden Street.

and warehouses multiplied, stretching ever deeper into the harbor. Even on the fringes, the workaday shipyards, rope walks, and fishermen's shanties jostled for space.

In this way, New England's complex and cosmopolitan Colonial economy shaped and was shaped by its landscape. Reinforced by the erratic landscape and bad roads, remote regions kept their own pace and clung to their seventeenth-century architectural identity. The more cosmopolitan seaward towns softened their Puritan attitudes toward both life and architecture. In Boston's North End, Colonel John Foster was copying the latest English mode for his mansion while Topsfield's Parson Capen still chose the medieval a scant twenty-one miles away.

England Architecture Comes of Age

surprise, then, that the winds of architectural e from England swept across the coastal towns The classical influence made its presence felt in the 1720s, first in the details—the scrolled nents, the quoins, the balustrades, translated English masonry into New England wood— inally in the proportions and attitudes towards e and composition—the flattening of the roof , the enlargement and regularity in doors and dows, the overall expansion for spacious halls and rways. By the Revolution, the sturdy homes of s American-Georgian style lined the streets of wport, Salem, Newburyport, Portsmouth, and a re of other towns. The Georgian trends and reli- ous mellowing touched even the traditional New ngland meetinghouse, where builders added grace- ul spires in the manner of Christopher Wren. The soaring shape became another symbol of New England for centuries to come.

Local building customs, settlement patterns, and decorative tradition altered the model slightly: compact half-houses and three-quarter houses in towns, foursquare farmhouses and Cape Cod cottages in the country. Nonetheless, whether it boasted a hip, gambrel, or bow roof, displayed flamboyant or austere carving, the outlines of Colonial architecture were fixed until after the Revolution.

The War of Independence eroded the Colonial face of the region. Towns worn by a quarter-century of stalled trade and war needed rebuilding. A new and prosperous merchant class set out to do so. The style appropriate to the wealth brought in by the emerging China trade would adorn that architecture, and a gifted architect facile with its forms would create it. Returning from England and France in 1787, Charles Bulfinch brought the modish Adamesque style to Boston. His elegant Massachusetts State House and magisterial homes for the merchant elite defined the architecture known as Federal.

The elegant attributes of this style, its attenuated proportions and delicate ornament, appealed to the sophisticated sensibilities of other coastal towns as well. From these, it traveled inland. Local carvers

Georgian architecture at its most elegant, the 1737 John Hancock house stood atop Beacon Hill, bringing a sophisticated interpretation of British styles to the colonies.

and builders like Samuel McIntire of Salem gave the style their own, often exquisite, stamp. In 1797, Asher Benjamin published *The Country Builder's Assistant.* The first American treatise on architecture, it sent the buildings of Bulfinch via Benjamin from the hub into the hinterlands. His pattern books and their successors would spread the New England image of hearth and home.

Slowly, the town landscape of New England took on a new look. Fine homes and substantial commercial and public buildings rose, first in the large towns, then in the small. Merchants fled the noisy waterfronts to build residential districts that some call America's first suburban retreats. High Street in Newburyport, Hillhouse Avenue in New Haven, Beacon Hill in Boston, and other enclaves boasted the architectural display. Public space also reflected the affluence. Civic-minded citizens planted trees on scruffy commons; town meetings voted to fill mudholes and ban geese and hogs from their ancient domains. Beautification had begun. The charm of the New England town green dates from these heady post-Revolutionary days.

The spirit of improvement went beyond aesthetics. In the towns, progressive merchants financed handsome wharves and warehouses. They also sponsored engineering feats—bridges, turnpikes, or waterways like Loammi Baldwin's Middlesex Canal— to connect them to the countryside. These "internal improvements" allowed the expansion that was to come. Here and there, too, along the Charles River at Waltham or the Blackstone River in Rhode Island,

Salem's Chestnut Street, a commanding avenue where builders shaped splendid mansions for the merchant princes of the East India trade.

New Englanders evolved an even more portentous building form. The textile mill began to spin the stuffs of a new industry. Yankee farmers turned from whittling and forging farm tools to devising water wheels and sluice gates, carding machines and belt-drives. New England's industrial revolution had begun.

Federal-era magnificence: the Nickels-Sortwell house in Wiscasset, Maine, built in 1807 for shipmaster Nickels, restored in 1900 by Mayor Sortwell of Cambridge, Massachusetts, and now owned by the Society for the Preservation of New England Antiquities.

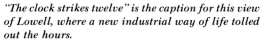
Industrial New England

In the beginning, in Pawtucket, for instance, factory builders adapted the forms they knew. They simply set two-story, gable-roofed frame or brick structures with regularly spaced windows at a convenient point on a fast-flowing river. Soon, however, the "manufactory" developed its own structural form and spun off a cluster of boardinghouses for the first "factory girls." The lone mill burgeoned into an architectural entourage. In Lowell, on the foamy waters of the Merrimack River near the entrance to the Middlesex Canal, the Boston Associates developed the model in the 1820s. A long chain of canals stepped down beside the factories to channel the water power; boardinghouses and tenements, company-built churches, meeting halls, and stores created a whole city. No more a simple structure by a tiny stream, the total milltown transformed the New England landscape. Within a few decades, milltowns lined the riverbanks in every New England state. Dense, massive, strong as stone, they fit into a grid or formal plan. Their design set them apart from the older New England architecturally; the pattern of life ordered by their factory bells set them apart socially. The industrial age was visible, audible, and real.

Hand in hand with the emerging industrial revolution came an expanding transportation revolution. The railroad met the needs of the Lowells and Manchesters. In the decades after its arrival in the 1830s, tracks crisscrossed the six states. Boston alone had ten terminals. Radiating from a hub, accelerating the

The famous "Lowell girls," farm women given inducements to turn the wheels of a new industry at Lowell, here seen in the detail of a bank note.

The age of rail created railroad stations across the six states. Some, like the Cornwall Bridge station in Cornwall, Connecticut, have become shops or vacation homes. Others simply vanished in the auto age.

pace of life in New England, shrinking the distances between towns, the railroad created a new scale of construction and new forms of architecture and landscape design. Railroad bridges, yards, and stations invaded the placid countryside. Ornate "railroad palaces," from Carpenter Gothic to massive Richardsonian monuments, became instant landmarks in the center of town. By the end of the century, nearly every town had its railroad depot. If the Puritan meetinghouse symbolized a theocratic, rural New England, the railroad station was totem to an industrialized, mobile one.

The railroad also created new living patterns. As the tracks fanned out, citydwellers soon discovered the advantages of commuting: work in the turbulent, smoky city, live in a placid suburban "villa." The concept flourished. Starting in the 1850s, horsedrawn street railways put suburban life within the means of working people. By the end of the century, electric trolleys expanded their reach. The rails sent New Englanders from their packed cities to the romantic "streetcar suburbs."

The centers too expanded. While natives headed out, their cities grew still denser: farm families drifted in from the countryside; Europe was sending New England the first of many waves of immigrants. From the 1840s, a flood of "New Americans" surged into Yankee New England, compacting the cities and milltowns they served. By 1875, the mill city of Holyoke, Massachusetts, had the second highest per-

The engaging eccentricities of the Mark Twain house in Hartford, Connecticut, were designed by Edward Tuckerman Potter; but even carpenter-builders could apply the Gothic detailing and Second Empire tower of this charming cottage in the same town.

centage of foreign-born residents in the United States, 52 percent of its population. Other towns felt the same swell.

Inevitably, as the region changed, so did construction techniques and materials. Balloon frames, the Chicago-bred rapid-fire building with lightweight supports nailed together, replaced heavy timber frames. Machine-made nails attached machine-planed moldings and machine-cut shingles to animate the façades of Victorian structures. Granite, pressed brick, cast iron, terra cotta entered the building repertoire.

Architectural pattern books, rolling ever faster off the mechanized presses, hastened the adoption of styles. Greek, Gothic, Italianate, French, Queen Anne, Romanesque, Stick Style, Shingle Style, tripped after one another in the panoply of Victorian models. Adapted by carpenter-builders, they adorned New England's towns. In sophisticated enclaves, a more self-conscious designer also appeared: the architect, an emerging professional, set lofty standards. Form-creators of national repute like A. J. Davis, Richard Morris Hunt, Henry Hobson Richardson, and McKim, Mead, and White, and regional talents like Henry Austin, Peabody and Stearns, and John Calvin Stevens, left a legacy of splendid structures to complement and inspire the everyday art of the carpenter-builder.

Arriving by train or steamer, urban New Englanders created a new landscape of repose and nostalgia on the old rural one. Here, the Station House, which greeted them in Durham, New Hampshire.

The Lure of the Old Landscape

By the end of the nineteenth century, a New Englander could scarcely see the earlier New England vista of small towns, neat farms, and scattered coastal cities. Yet here as nowhere else in the nation, old values endured. Even where "progress" forged across mill towns, business districts, or railroad-and-streetcar suburbs, tradition held sway. In the spare massing of the mills, in the restraint on Victorian eccentricities, in the green centers for planned industrial cities, the old endured amidst change.

The pell-mell rush bypassed some pockets altogether. Beneath the towering elms of Concord, Massachusetts, or Wethersfield, Connecticut, life went on much as before. Often, however, the ageless streetscape masked economic change. The eighteenth-century seaports no longer saw the returning seafarers, but welcomed the seasonal influx of artists, literati, and sightseers. The nineteenth-century "summer people" had begun to constitute a separate tribe.

Drawn to such places by their very anachronistic charm, the summer people, in turn, created their own picturesque landscape. In Martha's Vineyard, Kennebunkport, or Newport, they shaped clusters of "cottages" (be they two-room board-and-batten structures or the elegant behemoths of Newport, *cottage* was the term). The summer people's hankering for the past and their nostalgic evocation of its forms created an architecture of many modes.

In the mountains and countryside, the old landscapes changed subtly. With the stately decay wrought by the seasons, deserted homes and barns weathered into romantic ruins on their way to oblivion. The fields so arduously cleared reverted to woodland. Only the stone walls rolled on, sentinels from a vanished way of life. Farm towns now devoid of farmers turned to serving the "summer people," transforming house into inn, barn into summer theater, field into golf course. Chugging in with bags of city crinolines, booking on stagecoaches and wagons, the vacation folk headed ever further into the country to find the quaint, the old, the comfortable landscape of the past. In their eagerness to find it, they remade it.

Back in the winter cities, the same distress with the present and nostalgia for the past led them to look afresh at their grimy surroundings. Block upon block of depressed tenements blighted the lives of their inhabitants; forests of telephone poles and wires and jungles of trolley lines cluttered the scene. Didn't the great wealth and material progress of the age demand better of its environment? Didn't citydwellers need visual inspiration and respite? In the last quarter of the nineteenth century, Frederick Law Olmsted, creator of Central Park, emerged to ask and answer those questions for New England. Joined by others of the calling of "landscape architect" that he founded, Olmsted created parks, promenades, and boulevards. His Emerald Necklace, a network of green spaces, formed part of a total ecological plan

to link the urban and suburban parts of Boston. The greening of the hub had parallels in countless places: in parks for Hartford, Portland, Providence, New Haven; in old commons given new trees, monuments, fences; in splendid roads and integrated landscape plans. Olmsted's picturesque parks fell out of favor in the more formal City Beautiful era that followed, yet his heirs worked on, and the reforming spirit never faded. The Olmsted legacy of green space is a superb and, again, symbolic survivor on the landscape of today.

The Force Is Spent

For all the late-century beautification and building, the crush of new immigration from southern and eastern Europe still pressed New England. As the century turned, cities spilled into their suburbs; suburbs slid across farmlands. All this was as before. And yet, the great force that had once deployed the immigrant to transform New England was spent. Conservatism had seeped into the region's bones and eaten the marrow. The initiative that had laid the rails and piled high the mills deserted New England and moved south and west. In the decades after World War I, the textile and other industries—shoes, rubber, automobile parts, firearms, machine tools—followed the exodus. Gradually, the great network of railroad tracks which linked New England retreated. As the spur lines rusted among the weeds, New England slumbered. Building ceased.

The hyper-prosperity of the twenties never reached New England. Land booms happened elsewhere. Skyscrapers and their high-pitched, high-style architecture peaked outside the region. Save

for a few automobile showrooms, banks, and telephone buildings, precious few structures showed the sleek and flashy Art Deco and Streamline styles. Both modes celebrated a progress, prosperity, and modernism that eluded Jazz-Age New Englanders. Besides, New England had its style. The Colonial Revival mined a rich past and suited the conservative architectural taste of a generation making do with generations past.

Although New England barely partook of the boom of the twenties, it did share fully in the Depression that followed. Even the World War II growth spurt did not register for long on the landscape. At war's end, the region idled once again. Decline set in. Why did New England slide into economic despondence? What caused the region to languish? Was it the geography: a small-scale, patchy terrain hostile to the massive machinery and sweeping highways of the twentieth century? an industrial plant and corporate leadership grown senescent? Or had its work force grown too well-trained and assertive to do cheap labor or accept dull, automated jobs? Had the region's strengths become weaknesses in the rampant roughshod pace of the twentieth century? Was the ingrained conservatism of Puritan days, for good or ill, unable to accept modern vanities?

Whatever the reasons, most of the accoutrements of modern life came slowly to twentieth-century New England. For almost a quarter of a century, modern life escaped New England; or perhaps New England escaped modern life. Drive-in movies, supermarkets, shopping centers, superhighways, the aesthetic detritus of mid-century America, all seeped in slowly. Long before the "preservation movement" took hold, poverty helped preserve New England.

Art Deco in an Orono, Maine, diner. Here and there, New England displayed a modest version of the flashy style of the 1920s.

The businessman in his "dated" warehouse, the rural family in an "obsolete" Victorian farmhouse could not afford the shiny market or the sprawling ranch home of the latest American dream. "Use it up/wear it out/make it do/or do without" reigned perforce.

Eventually, of course, New England succumbed, embracing, or embraced by, the new. Come the end of the war, federally funded highways bulldozed their way straight through the recalcitrant old topography. Federally financed mortgages planted the "split-levels" and "Cape Cods" of Anywhere, U.S.A., in fields and meadows. Shopping centers, gas stations, and franchises spread asphalt across the land. In cities, Washington-funded urban renewal gouged huge holes in the historic fabric to insert some concrete or glass civic center or government building. In a few cases, noted architects rendered valid twentieth-century designs. More often, this second-hand International Style hurt.

The Leading State of Mind

In the 1960s and 1970s, that most ancient New England trait, Yankee ingenuity, seemed to awaken from its long hibernation to transform the New England economy once more. This time it was electronics. High-tech industries replaced the vanished blue-collar ones. Route 128, birthplace of a new industry, circled Boston. Its pattern of an interlocked ring of highways, industry, and suburban buildings, soon radiated into the New England countryside.

By the time this latest "New England Renaissance" filtered downtown, another urban ethos had evolved. Times and tastes had changed. Communities, disenchanted with urban renewal, had banded to stop the bulldozer. Cities and neighborhoods had defenders. The preservation movement was underway. Revitalization had supplanted renewal. Build-

ings bequeathed by earlier generations were "recycled." A latter-day gentry felt the pull of the culture of downtown. A passion for old buildings and plenty of them made New England the center for a major shift to their refurbishment.

Meanwhile, economics and energy-consciousness came together. The energy crisis damaged New England. In an energy-dependent era, the shortage of gas and oil combined with the cold winters that had plagued the Puritan settlers to challenge the ingenuity of their descendants. Concern for energy-efficiency made the glass-walled boxes of the sixties obsolete and recalled the days of center chimneys and sheltered dooryards. Phrases like *energy retrofitting* sounded in the city; woodstoves and woodpiles populated the countryside. The energy effects in the seventies only intensified the outlines of change already sketched. The romance of the superhighway had paled. Older neighborhoods closer to the cities revived, while the rising costs of new construction made rehabilitation more feasible. The revived passion for the past even colored new construction: Post-Modernism, a reworking of historic forms, edged out more minimal modes.

Computers and woodstoves, slick industrial parks and refurbished downtowns, a restored foursquare Colonial with solar collectors on the back. Will a boom economy destroy an ingrained sense of austerity? New England's prosperity, however tenuous, has raised questions. Can architectural growth coexist with the heritage that defines New England? That heritage goes beyond the buildings and landscapes of three and a half centuries to a historic attitude: "Use it up, wear it out . . . ," the Puritan concept of stewardship, Yankee ingenuity, the beauty of the practical. Once again, New England, in its architectural landscape as in its life, must look to the past to find guidance for the future.

The vast plaza and concrete cubism of the new City Hall and burgeoning highrises contrast with the historic architecture of Boston.

Commemoration and celebration as a way of life in New England: a nineteenth-century view of the obelisk at Concord, installed in 1836 to celebrate the Revolution.

2. The Preserving of New England

A capital from Governor Hutchinson's mansion in Boston. In 1834, wreckers tore down the North End structure but cared enough to save this decorative element, a sign of an early, if fragmented, appreciation of New England's history.

hy here? Why did preservation begin in New England? To other Americans, the New World was a clean slate awaiting the inscription of a new people, not an etched tablet to preserve and protect. What made the New Englander come to value the past?

From their first days in the Promised Land, the people of these six states knew that they had a history with meaning beyond themselves. As time passed they built the Cradle of Liberty and they stood their ground at Lexington. Surely they had an obligation to maintain this historic legacy on the landscape. Through the decades, that caring for a particular moment in time translated into caring for the historic landscape that held it.

The preservation of words on paper came first. Salvaging the history held in documents launched a concern for saving New England's heritage. Inevita-

bly, perhaps, it started with the work of two men of the cloth. Jeremy Belknap and William Bentley, both heirs to the Puritan passion for history, began keeping records not long after the War of Independence.

Dr. William Bentley, the portly clergyman of Salem's East Church, filled four volumes with his diary. An unceasing scribe, he noted houses demolished and docks constructed. Though the good doctor found, described, and ruminated upon the meaning of artifacts of Colonial days, Belknap's work meant more. A Dover, New Hampshire, minister with erudition beyond his pastorate, Belknap spent much of his twenty years there compiling the three-volume *History of New Hampshire,* published from 1784 to 1792. Then he moved to Boston, there too hoarding historical documents and saving fragile Revolutionary papers from oblivion. This visionary preservationist had the

Looking Backward

Why this quickened interest in the past? For one thing, by the 1830s the past had accumulated: New England had clocked in two centuries of history, and simultaneously recorded losses of the visible mementos of that history. Material prosperity, improved communications, and an influx of fashions in architecture and lifestyle had begun to shatter the region's comfortable stability. Belknap, Bentley, and those who followed watched the past vanishing. "I grieved to see the connection between the past and the present century so entirely lost," Bentley said, mourning the death of an elderly bachelor and the furnishings soon to be stripped from his ancient house. The pace of change only quickened.

This grief was not simply nostalgia. New Englanders also worried about their loss of power within the nation. Settlers streamed south and west. The Louisiana Purchase, which doubled the size of the United States, shrank New England's place in it. Meanwhile, "Mr. Jefferson's Embargo" and "Mr. Madison's War" destroyed the region's trade. Its people sensed their waning strength. Documenting and celebrating the roots of their greatness reassured them.

The fiftieth anniversary of the beginnings of the Revolution intensified the look backward. Fourth of July orators dwelt on buildings and places harking to Revolutionary days. Patriotic sentiment swelled, and monuments rose. In 1836 Emerson hymned the "rude bridge that arched the flood" of the embattled farmers; thousands came to Concord to view the historic spot. Obelisks rose on hallowed sites here as at Bunker Hill.

New England's mid-nineteenth-century literary renaissance heightened this retrospection. Lament-

more systematic approach, the broader outlook, and, by creating the Massachusetts Historical Society in 1791, the greater impact. The first in the country, the society fulfilled Belknap's dream of a safe place to hold "dead materials for the use of a future historian." Repository for documents, center for scholarly study, the society was able "to show the secret springs" of New England history, as John Adams commented. Joined in 1848 by the Essex Institute in Dr. Bentley's Salem, the society laid the foundations for preservation.

The society's rich and venerable archives were only the vanguard of a movement, however. Devoted students of bygone days from small towns like Lynn, Barnstable, and Newbury wrote histories in the 1820s and 1830s, and now and again their newspapers and magazines began to carry odd items of historical interest, too.

ing the difficulty of writing great literature in a country so new it had "no shadows," Hawthorne, Emerson, Longfellow, and others searched New England's past for events to create a chiaroscuro America. Hawthorne especially found the dimensions of days gone by in the Puritan heritage. An intervening century had shrouded Puritan lives with the requisite shadows. The Concord author's books popularized the romantic image of the early New England house, a version of his own "Old Manse," cloaked by ancient wisteria vines and lilacs, its weathered clapboards sheltering dramatic tales of bygone days.

Nostalgia is a twentieth-century staple, but to a nineteenth-century nation of the new, the hankering for antiquity was novel. Americans still looked to the future, romanticizing untrammeled landscapes. "Where the wolf roams, the plow shall glisten," painter Thomas Cole wrote. "On the gray crag shall rise temple and tower; mighty deeds shall be done in the yet pathless wilderness. . . ." While Manifest Destiny still beckoned Americans westward, the stories of remote days by New England writers worked on the region's imagination: New England's "shabby" buildings took on the aura of sacred keepsakes.

The industrial revolution heightened this nostalgia. New Englanders suffered the crowding, mechanization, and pollution, the uprooting of lives and the scarring of landscapes by "progress," before other Americans. Inevitably, they clung to the world obliterated by this first surge of modernism. Predictably, they led in attempts to preserve its remains.

Thoreau uttered the most famous excoriation of material progress in 1854 in *Walden*. He was not alone. Other voices joined the Concord naturalist. George Perkins Marsh, a Vermont sheep raiser and lumber dealer turned congressman and diplomat, published *Man and Nature* a decade later. A conser-

vationist before the word appeared, Marsh recalled the overlumbering that had destroyed the ecology of his native state in the 1830s. Resources are not inexhaustible, he declared. They must be husbanded carefully. *Man and Nature* became a foundation for the modern conservation movement. Marsh also shared in the design of the Washington Monument and Vermont's capitol. His sense of stewardship for the whole environment, cityscape and countryside,

A celebrated 1848 daguerreotype captures Deerfield's Old Indian House at the time when early preservationists rallied to stop its destruction.

would characterize New England's caretakers for generations to come.

If writers and intellectuals guided the way, other New Englanders followed. Inspired, no doubt, by summer readings of Hawthorne and Longfellow, they pursued the quaint, the picturesque, the historical; and they found them in Portsmouth and Newport and Cape Ann, in the hills of Lenox and on the shores of Maine. The nostalgic quest of these latter-day villagers amplified the work of local historians and fueled future architectural shifts as well. The travels of two architectural students during the 1870s had later repercussions. Stanford White and Charles Follen McKim's summer with their sketchbooks along the New England coast produced endless pages of early New England houses. The drawings would both stimulate the Colonial Revival and serve as source material for restoring the genuine article. With the celebration of the centennial in 1876, the attention paid to historic architecture grew.

Preservation versus Progress

The deepening appeal of the past also promoted an impulse to preserve its living symbols. As early as mid-century, the drive to save the Old Indian House in Deerfield became the first cause célèbre of preservation in New England. That struggle ended in failure, but the crusade took its place in the epic of preservation battles and powered later victories.

A lone survivor of the Indian raid of 1704, the Old Indian House had become a local curiosity even by 1847. Neighbors found the structure endearing and the owner's plans to flatten it for a modern replace-

Bostonians fought to save the old Hancock house, next to the State House, and published this broadside, but to no avail.

ment appalling. Newspapers publicized the controversy. Townspeople friendly to its charm and history even summoned a special town meeting and produced the first preservation broadside in American history to publicize it. To no avail. Supporters could not raise $2,000 to buy the house, nor collect the scant $150 needed to move it. The owner tore it down. In death, the Old Indian House became a rallying cry: "A tragedy which must not happen again!"

It did happen again, though. In 1863, perhaps the finest Colonial mansion in New England joined the list of lost buildings. Governor John Hancock's home had overlooked Boston Common for 126 years when the Hancock heirs offered the property for sale, first to the state, then to the city. Bogged down in technicalities and governmental sluggishness, both failed to respond. The building fell. Again, surviving in its demise, the Hancock house shaped the preservation movement in New England for a century. Dismayed by the inability of government agencies to thwart demolition, Yankee preservationists learned they must rely on themselves. New Haven's razing of its old State Capitol building in 1889 reinforced the decision. In the future, they would depend on private, not public, means to save their heritage.

The success of such private efforts in the next two battles in Boston justified that self-sufficient stance. The historic Old South Meeting House, where the Boston Tea Party had brewed, came first. Despite its dramatic escape from the flames of Boston's Great Fire in 1872, the vacant building seemed doomed a few years later. Rapid downtown development threatened it. Demolition crews drew near. Workmen had even mounted ladders and begun to extract the clock from its historic tower when help appeared. On June 11, 1876, a clothing dealer bought the right to keep the building standing for seven days.

From this dramatic but tenuous beginning, the movement took hold. Three days later, Wendell Phil-

lips stirred a mass meeting to save "the very spot where bold men spoke." Led and financed by the Brahmin women whose heirs would head the roster of preservation's warriors, spurred on by rallies with Emerson, Oliver Wendell Holmes, and other luminaries, a citizens' committee formed. It turned the short reprieve into permanent salvation. The saving of the Old South became, in the words of historian Walter Muir Whitehall, "the first instance in Boston where responsibility for the historic heritage of the city triumphed over considerations of profit, expediency, laziness and vulgar convenience." It also became the first instance of the alliance of elite and ordinary citizens that would characterize the region's preservation efforts.

Scarcely had the Meeting House crisis ended, however, when its success prompted a second major battle to restore the abused Old State House nearby. Fired again by the building's links to the Revolution (plus, perhaps, Chicago's attempt to buy and move the building to fill that city's historic void), Bostonians rallied. The city, landlord to the commercialized and disfigured Revolutionary relic, must do better by it, they insisted. In 1882, restoration was secured with city funds.

Sparked by such visible victories, towns across New England campaigned to hold on to their own historic houses. From the Wadsworth-Longfellow house in Portland in 1901 to the Jared Coffin house in Nantucket, finally saved in 1928, more and more New Englanders hoarded the old in the face of the advancing new.

Revolutionary links inspired New Englanders to preserve such eighteenth-century houses as this, the Webb-Deane-Stevens complex in Wethersfield, Connecticut, where the Yorktown Conference between George Washington and the Count de Rochambeau was held.

Looking to the Landscape

Green space also benefited from such sentiments. In the decades after the Civil War, a sprucing, even a mythologizing, of the historic landscape followed. The tattered Lexington Green was groomed, the Litchfield Common "restored," the mall in Newburyport beautified. The same literary, academic, and nostalgic patricians who articulated the case for architectural salvation espoused outdoor enthusiasms as well, forming the Appalachian Mountain Club in 1876 and the Audubon Club ten years later. The crusading that created the western parks had parallels across the region.

At times, the conservation cause paralleled the preservation one; still more often it shared its prophets. A concern for the complete metropolis, city and

Deerfield's quiet beauties remained constant, aided by some of the earliest historic-house lovers.

country, stirred Charles Eliot to plan a total metropolitan park system for the Hub. The landmark Trustees of Public Reservations, which he founded in 1891, would have still more influence, leading to the creation of England's National Trust (on which America's National Trust for Historic Preservation was patterned in the next century).

As the century closed, it was understandable that preservationists and conservationists alike sought to stay the darker side of "progress," for progress was grim indeed in New England. The announcement with the 1890 census of the closing of the frontier startled Westerners, but it only confirmed what New Englanders sensed at home—their landscape was shrinking. They must cling to it. Though joined to antimodernism and to more negative feelings toward the new immigrants, the impulse to preserve had positive motivations as well. It shared in the progressive urge to reform a world trampled by rampant technology. What historian Charles Hosmer would later call the battle of "growth vs. beauty" had begun. The landscape, whether imbued with scenic splendor or endowed with architectural wonders, drew still more devotees.

Curating the Past

The old town of Ipswich, Massachusetts, supplied the setting for a new pattern in preserving the past. Here, in the 1890s, another history-conscious cleric led the way. The Reverend Thomas Franklin Waters persuaded the Ipswich Historical Society to buy, move, and painstakingly restore a seventeenth-century structure, the John Whipple house, not for its role in any historic event, not for any personal associations, but for its architectural value as an example of early Colonial building. It was, said Waters,

"a link that binds us to the remote Past and to a solemn and earnest manner of living, quite in contrast with much in our modern life." An America in flux needed such roots. New England's historic architecture, like its natural landscape, was secure and good.

The growing interest in old houses as architectural specimens of a stable past prompted questions: How had the houses originally looked? How had people lived in them? Curiosity heightened. Research, and the collection of artifacts and pictures, followed. Soon New Englanders became intrigued with two ways of displaying the answers to those questions: the period room and the outdoor museum of folk life.

The person who popularized these European-bred ideas here was "a man of prodigious energy and multiple talents." As a freewheeling enthusiast and secretary of the Essex Institute from 1898 to 1919, George Francis Dow set up three "typical Colonial" period rooms. He took a kitchen, a parlor, and a bedroom, their woodwork and furnishings drawn from a single point in time, and tucked them inside the Salem institution. Then, looking outside, Dow saw an endangered building, the 1685 John Ward house. He moved it onto the Institute's grounds and fitted it out with an "Old Salem" apothecary, a "cent shop" (general store), and a weaving room, the way he visualized them. Finally, in hopes of "giving much of an atmosphere of livability," Dow stationed costumed hostesses to guide visitors through the house. The periodization of history had arrived. Although Dow did not invent the period room, his flair popularized it; the installation was a hit—and a model. Dow himself later enlarged upon it for the state's tercentenary, creating Pioneer Village, an enclave of thatched huts in Salem. Other museums followed suit with re-created rooms and villages isolating historic periods. The old houses, staged with figures in period dress and photographed by Wallace Nutting to romanticize and popularize bygone days, testified to the appeal of this past.

This burgeoning collection and interpretation of history within a museum setting, however, also led to the first schism in the drive to preserve the past. Intent on saving and exhibiting America's built heritage, museums now charged in to "rescue" threatened architecture. But should museum people, as proposed, drag the Wentworth-Gardner house in Portsmouth, New Hampshire, to the Metropolitan Museum in New York? However imperfect the treatment, however much smaller the audience, shouldn't a building stay rooted in the soil from which it arose?

Emotions ran high on such issues, inflamed by regional pride and resentment: the affluent collectors versus the locals. The debates that raged over the Wentworth-Gardner house and Henry Ford's forays into New England to gather structures for his Greenfield Village in Dearborn, Michigan, would not die. From these early controversies sprang the numerous branches of historic preservation that still exist today: the house museum, the museum village, museum interpretation of architecture and the decorative arts, even historic districts and the revitalization of worn buildings and places. The questions raised remain pertinent: To whom does our architectural heritage belong? For whom should it be preserved? For what purpose? And what, indeed, does the term *preserve* mean?

Appleton Oversees a Region

The father figure who would address such questions and shape New England preservation in a broader way also belonged to the Brahmin elite that tried to stay the evil forces of the century. A Bostonian of independent means, eccentric habits, and somewhat delicate health, William Sumner Appleton devoted his life to saving New England's past. Imbued with a "visionary" belief that old buildings belonged in their original settings, he worked to keep them there. His earnest letters—opposing the removal of a building or arguing that a doorway or room of choice paneling or wallpaper should stay intact—had impact. But Appleton wanted more. Frustrated by the narrow purpose and limited resources of the house-by-house approach, he sought a far-reaching method: he found it in a regional preservation organization. In 1910, the zealous guardian of

William Sumner Appleton on the steps of the Harrison Gray Otis house in 1922. An awesome figure in the annals of preservation, he led the way by bringing new uses to such buildings as the Abraham Browne house in Watertown, Massachusetts.

New England's heritage began the Society for the Preservation of New England Antiquities. At its helm for thirty-seven years, he honed the tools and tenets of New England preservation.

Appleton's goal for the society was self-sufficiency; he aimed to preserve historic properties by buying, restoring, and operating them on a self-sustaining basis. Within a year, the society acquired its first building. By Appleton's death in 1947, it owned more than fifty. The energetic collector did not want to turn all old houses into museums, however; he merely wanted to preserve them. He therefore advocated renting historic homes to sympathetic tenants who would open them to the public from time to time. He also invented new uses for them—a tea room and gift shop to support the restored Abraham Browne house in Watertown, Massachusetts, for instance. By such means, Appleton found economic life for old architecture. He pioneered and practiced "adaptive reuse" fifty years before its vogue.

Appleton was also a pioneer in documenting and restoring old buildings. Conservative in restoration, he advocated saving all traces of the past, both ancient and recent. Unlike his peers, he refrained from fabricating the appearance of an earlier age. In pursuit of documentation, he collected the old photographs, artifacts, and documents that became the foundation for the society's research collections, and he encouraged such collections elsewhere. In the end, the man synonymous with New England preservation for four decades left the region one of its most creative and influential organizations. Appleton professionalized preservation: he raised the level of knowledge everywhere.

The art of documentation also got a boost during the Depression from the federal government. Created as a New Deal work project, the Historic

American Buildings Survey (HABS) recorded historic buildings through drawings, measurements, and photographs. Alas, such paper preservation did not save the buildings it recorded: 21 of 190 Bay State structures recorded in the survey's first year had disappeared by its third. Nine that stood in one small part of Newburyport came down for a highway. Such figures gave dimension to the anguish and urgency preservationists had long felt, but the thirties still brought little activism in the public sphere. While conservationists enlisted the New Deal for land reclamation, forests, and parks, preservationists remained private and elitist, their independence insular.

Enclaves of the Past

During this same period, the museum village took on a new importance. From the 1920s, the scale of these villages grew enormously. The idea of Colonial Williamsburg, the Rockefeller-backed enclave

The past, fabricated afresh at Plimoth Plantation or transported to Old Sturbridge Village or Mystic Seaport (seen here), failed to stem the destruction of the genuine historic landscape.

pieced together by New England architects Perry, Dean, Shaw and Hepburn with landscape architect Arthur Shurcliff, spread up north. Throughout the 1930s, wealthy New Englanders created more village enclaves. Ambitious to duplicate bygone and better days, collectors planted artifacts and historic architecture at Old Sturbridge Village in Massachusetts,

Mystic Seaport in Connecticut, and the Shelburne Museum in Vermont. In the 1950s, local boosters even fabricated a complete village at Plimoth Plantation in Plymouth. The opening of these preserves drew crowds who shared their creators' urge to recall a simpler and, to them, better America.

Soothing as the vision they evoked, such preserves of the past could not save the landscape around them. The fabric of New England's heritage was eroding. Besieged by rapid change, plagued by urban attrition, the next decade saw another generation of preservationists turn their energies beyond what Whitehill called "well-walled illusions within which the visitor may enjoy a synthetic past." Inspired by Charleston and New Orleans, Bay Staters formed the region's first two historic preservation districts—one on Nantucket and one on Boston's Beacon Hill—by 1955. A year later, preservationists in Providence, Rhode Island, began the comprehensive survey which led to the creation of the College Hill district in 1960. That same year, Massachusetts simplified the process for other communities by passing legislation enabling local governments to create historic districts. Connecticut lawmakers followed in 1961.

Such labors did not come easily. As an extension of land-use zoning (the right of the government to regulate the use of private property for the public good), historic districts were virtually guaranteed to produce controversy. In this land of life, liberty, and the pursuit of happiness through private property, the government was limiting landholders' freedom. They had precedent, of course: Hadn't the first town magistrates dictated the design of chimneys to protect towns from fire? Why, then, couldn't their heirs stop demolition of historic buildings and regulate their alteration, to guard the town's beauty and heritage? Controversial or not, the district law worked. It changed the rules. No longer must lovers of build-

Boston's Beacon Hill, the quintessential and first historic district in New England, retains its traditional charm along sloping ways like Acorn Street.

ings own them to save them. The law had come to their aid. Embedded in that law was an assumption basic to preservation—that the public has as much right to an environment with aesthetic and historic value as it does to health and safety.

Thus fortified, historic districts spread slowly across the region. By the 1980s, the Bay State alone could count a hundred zones of protected buildings. Beyond the territorial gain was a philosophical one: For the first time, New Englanders had ventured beyond the private approach. They had enlisted government in their battle to save the environment.

The Battle Escalates

Roping off such historic districts went far beyond roping off museum villages. Nonetheless, this scale, too, began to seem insignificant amidst the dismantling of the larger landscape after World War II. In the wake of the Depression and the war, a building boom unequaled in history swept across the country. Everywhere the agents of the new ousted the old, but the effect on this oldest corner of the country was especially brutal. The nineteenth-century Peterboro Tavern in Peterboro, New Hampshire, fell for a bank. A concrete-and-asphalt shopping center chewed into elegant Bellevue Avenue in Newport. Examples proliferated; the handsome but outmoded remains of better days lay in ruins.

But the loss of this or that building dimmed in the devastation that followed the Federal Highway Act of 1956 and the urban-renewal legislation a year later. Empowered to carry out projects on a scale hitherto unimagined, highway agencies cut vast swaths through countryside, village, and town. Urban renewal ravaged so-called slums, flattened decayed but striking architecture, and riddled the region's cities. Portland's Union Railroad Station, Boston's India and T wharves, Manchester's Amos-

keag Mills, all became casualties of an ethos that defined "sixty-mile-an-hour architecture" as good, old buildings as bad.

The fabric of three centuries was in shreds. Preservation, as defined in the last century's labors, had salvaged little. Impotent against the federal firestorm, its elite had fought mere brushfires: What did it matter that a museum or single building was saved by a mini-band of afficionados? As the economics changed, even the venerable Society for the Preservation of New England Antiquities could not support the structures it had so painstakingly preserved. House museums and villages struggled to survive leaky roofs, worn stairs, rotting beams. Meanwhile, a century after the demise of the Old Indian House and John Hancock's mansion, the cry of "a tragedy which must not happen again" sounded almost monthly. By the 1960s, more than one-third of the buildings surveyed by the Historic American Building Survey in the thirties had fallen. Had the urge to preserve and protect come to naught?

Reviving the Sense of Stewardship

The answer was "not quite," for a new generation felt the sense of escalating crisis. Intensifying and shifting their tactics, activists focused on government as the source of the problem and the solution alike. They banded to fight what Martin Anderson would label "the federal bulldozer."

Once more, New England writers broached the issue as a moral one. Again, Boston, a hub of intellect and activism, prompted two of the most powerful tracts. In the 1960s, Jane Jacobs's *The Death and Life of Great American Cities* made the city's North End a classic case for old neighborhoods where lively stoops and low-scale structures kept "eyes on the street." Herbert Gans's *The Urban Villagers* traced the ethnic enclave eradicated in Boston's West End

In the early 1960s, Jane Jacobs argued that such gritty neighborhoods as Boston's North End were not "slums" to eradicate but vital urban centers.

and alerted the nation to the shame of its destruction. Writers in a special issue of *Daedalus* might still call the sixties the "Post-City Age," but many of the people who lived in those cities felt a sense of urban revival.

In the environmental movement, vision broadened, too. As preservationists expanded from saving single buildings to salvaging whole neighborhoods, conservationists, stirred by Rachel Carson's *Silent Spring,* shifted from protecting stands of trees or single species to protecting the total environment and its inhabitants. The attitude of America began to change. Gradually, what David Brower called "homage to the great god growth," faded. Environmentalists led the way, securing a long list of land-use and conservation laws that would serve the built along with the natural environment.

Stewards of the historic environment also looked to Washington. *With Heritage So Rich,* a report sponsored by the Conference of Mayors and written by Walter Muir Whitehill and others, reinforced political pressure for federal action. Together they generated the National Historic Preservation Act of 1966. This landmark act changed the ground rules for preservation from the top down, expanding the defini-

tion of the National Register of Historic Places to include structures of local significance, and encouraging state historic preservation offices. In one stroke, the act created both a broad definition of what should be preserved and a federal and state bureaucracy to act on these decisions. Preservationists at last had a beachhead within the government. Regulation by regulation, appropriation by appropriation, they fought to expand both their territory and their arsenal of weapons.

In the next two decades, the SHPOs—State Historic Preservation Officers—and their enlarging staffs served as agents for an enlarging constituency of preservationists. From the five workers sandwiched between a McDonald's and a Dunkin' Donuts in business-first New Hampshire to the staff of twenty-nine handsomely quartered in more sensitive Massachusetts, the SHPOs watchdogged historic sites, carrying out environmental reviews and administering federal grant and tax-incentive programs. Local commissions grew in size and multiplied their programs, surveying and designating properties, preventing their demolition or poor alteration. In a nation of laissez-faire development, activists took advantage of these new powers, sometimes the only powers at hand, to protect the environment against real estate speculators or highway blunderbusses. Now when highway agents menaced the historic Battle Road in Concord or Lexington, protectors could martial a new set of laws.

After decades of defending the barricades by themselves, the Brahmin heirs of the Old South's defenders—the clichéd "little old ladies in tennis shoes"—no longer stood alone. A legion of allies joined them to fight for preservation. Armed with surveys, lawsuits, and environmental-impact statements to stay the wreckers, bolstered by the public sentiment on their side, groups like the Hartford Architectural Conservancy could use everything from

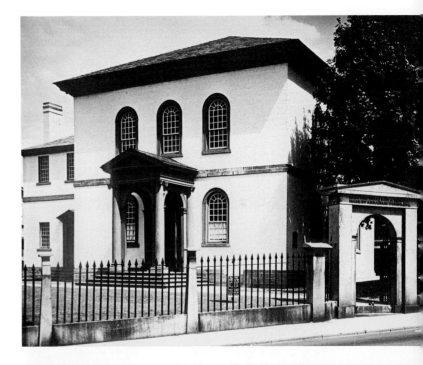

As costs rise, the National Park Service helps keep a roof over historic buildings run by private groups. Here, Newport's Touro Synagogue, designed by Peter Harrison.

"guerrilla" to political tactics. Fighting to stop Route 101 in the Monadnock region of New Hampshire or battling to protect Waterbury's nineteenth-century downtown from demolition, advocates adapted such tools to stop the bulldozer. Fortified with skills in recycling and restoration, they used them to refurbish Burlington's Flynn Theater and Cambridge's Bulfinch Courthouse. Everywhere today, new allies emerge, and old ones regroup. A Friends of the Public Garden coalesces to champion a precious public landscape; an Ottauquechee Land Trust organizes to protect farm land; SPNEA becomes more public. All the while, New England's ubiquitous schools hone students' skills, teaching them to do everything from devise master plans to analyze paint samples.

Today, the stewardship of New England belongs to more and more people. What Jeremy Belknap and William Bentley started, thousands spread. The curator restoring an architectural gem, the lawyer crafting conservation easements, the conservationist charting damage to the region's ecosystem from acid rain, and the neighborhood association combating arson and abandonment are all their heirs.

And yet, this world of endless coalitions also holds endless contradictions. For, as the preservation movement entered the mainstream, it absorbed the conflicting currents of a pluralistic society. As hardheaded business practice came to the aid of history, it permeated—tainted, some say—the purist ideals. With so many developers adopting preservation and so many preservationists adopting bottom-line goals, it has become hard to tell the sheep from the goats—or, some would argue, from the wolves-in-

Still a leader in preserving New England, the Society for the Preservation of New England Antiquities (SPNEA) now includes a modern house, the home of Bauhaus master Walter Gropius, in its definition of historic architecture and provides a wider range of services in its educational and consulting programs.

sheep's-clothing. One person's preservation is another's intrusion; one's neighborhood revitalization is another's gentrification. Complex needs breed conflicting constituencies.

For all the differences, in the 1980s search to save what William Whyte called *The Last Landscape,* the demons remain the same: the Great God Progress and the Great Monster Growth have not ended their assault on the built and natural environment. In an era of pervasive change, the work of the guardians of New England seems ever more imperative. Protectors of the battered but still beautiful landscape of New England, they overlap, they intermingle, sometimes they conflict. In common, though, they share a sense of urgency and identity: they are New Englanders preserving New England.

Preservation means construction and reconstruction. Here, the creation of columns for the restoration of Bulfinch's Courthouse in Cambridge, Massachusetts, and the fabrication of handmade waterstruck bricks at the Royal River Brickyard in Yarmouth, Maine.

PART TWO
Saving the Town and Cityscape

The still-peaceful coves of Monhegan, Maine.

3. Waterfronts: Down to the Seashore and Riverside

*B*y history and destiny, New England was water-born, water-bred, and water-bound. From the beginning, the coves and rivers threading in and out of the coast of the North Atlantic harbored a people joined to wind and tide. "We breathed the air of foreign countries, curiously interblended with our own," Lucy Larcom wrote of her New England girlhood in Beverly, Massachusetts, in the 1800s. "Men talked about a voyage to Calcutta, or Hong Kong, or up the Straits—meaning Gibraltar and the Mediterranean—as if it were not much more than going to the next village."

The tang of salt still flavors New England's language. Yankees go "down" to Maine and "up" to Boston, a reflection not of geography but of the way the wind blows; and when a job needs doing, they "turn to." The landscape of the New England coast bears the imprint of

Figurehead of a clipper ship, now at the Peabody Museum in Salem.

this seafaring past: The sea captains' houses with their "widow's walks" line compact coastal towns. Lighthouses beam from rocky promontories. Granite warehouses stand solid above their pilings, fronted by a thicket of masts.

At closer range, changes color the view. The sign on the house door reads, CAPTAIN LORD MANSION. OPEN TUES.–SUN., 2–4 P.M. A tourist with a camera lines up a shot of the lighthouse. The smell of broiling hamburger wafts from the warehouse, and the swaying masts belong to "Sou' westers" and "Sea Sprites" whose sometime crews toast the sunset with gin-and-tonics.

As the world moved from whale oil to gas light to electricity, from salt cod to canned tuna to frozen fishsticks, from clipper ships to railroads to air freight, the economy of New England's waterfront shifted. The uses that gave it life atrophied. In countless towns, the vital

harbor center eroded into a worn edge. In some seaports like Boston and Portland, the waterfront decayed into a seedy shell of its old self; in others, like New Haven and Providence, it vanished altogether, as lost as Atlantis under the fill and buildings. Highways, seeking turf, further walled off the view; and, as time passed, those who lived there could scarcely recollect that their drydocked landscape once sprang from the sea.

In the sixties and seventies, the tide of awareness turned. Artists and other maritime pioneers saw the water's edge as a "room with a view" and moved in; planners and developers followed. As shipping and fishing fell off, the "industry" to which New England's waterfront renewers turned was recreation.

Anachronistic or not, the square-rigger still carries magic in its sails. Mystic Seaport in Connecticut draws 450,000 visitors a year to its semblance of an old-time waterfront. In 1976, thousands crowded the shores and jammed the windows of Boston's towers for sightings of the Tall Ships. In towns and cities along the coast, the lure of the harbor's wharves and warehouses, sheds and shanties, and the narrow streets of snug homes unreeling behind them is scarcely less compelling. An age daunted by the slick and ephemeral finds charm in the worn and weathered, in wharfside wood and stone, water-blackened by the centuries. Cities compacted by walls of masonry value this expansive landscape, an open space and window on nature's world.

So potent is seaside charm today that even those towns that had lost all sense of their waterfronts have begun to resurrect them. Burlington, Vermont, has allocated twenty-six acres along Lake Champlain and debates plans to develop them; the rubble-strewn, dilapidated Brewery Square site on New Haven's Quinnipac riverfront has had a $14 million rebirth; and Providence now envisions burying whole highways. "Ripping the lid off the Providence River," the

Providence Journal described plans to revive 4.5 miles of riverfront. Whether rebuilding a vanished heritage or refurbishing a neglected one, these communities are reclaiming their waterfronts, not as places to work but as places to play.

In some towns, the pleasure-seekers and the working waterfront live in relative harmony. In Gloucester, Massachusetts, day-trippers drawn to the "Gateway to the Whales" and painters looking for the picturesque still share space with fishermen. In Castine, Maine, the training ship and contemporary quarters of the Maine Maritime Academy lend a note of authenticity to connect the picturesque with the real. The workaday forms of ships and cranes in the fifty-four-acre Bath Iron Works thrust above the horizon on the Kennebec River in Maine, signaling the ongoing work of the sea.

Elsewhere, though, the tide of tourism has all but washed away the real salt. For all the delight of Camden, Maine, or Stonington, Connecticut, the loss of the real romance of the sea for a Valentine version has diminished New England's waterside world.

A sense of magic and retreat lies in the mist of the Connecticut River marina at Brattleboro, Vermont, where a restaurant caters to those who return to New England's waterfront.

Waterfront renaissance: Providence, Rhode Island, covered its upper harbor (shown here in 1900) but now plans to unearth its buried waters with a $38 million development plan.

"You knew the waterfront was gone when you couldn't see rails and you couldn't buy breakfast at breakfast time, which is six o'clock," says Boston Harbor Associates director Thom Ennen, mourning the loss of genuine seafaring life along Boston's waterfront.

Nantucket's Second Life

Consider Nantucket, the classic of made-over coastal towns—a slumbering seaport roused by tourists. Whaling built Nantucket. From the seventeenth century through the nineteenth, island sailors chased the giant sea mammals from the Arctic to the South Pacific. The memorabilia at the Whaling Museum testifies to the maritime origins in row upon row of harpoons, prints of sailing ships, and scrimshaw. With the introduction of kerosene in the 1840s, the market for whale oil disappeared. The whaling ships lay idle at the wharves. Their owners retreated to the Greek-porticoed mansions along Main Street, emerging to swap sea stories in the Pacific Club at the head of Straight Wharf. For a hundred years, young, more ambitious islanders left the town's quiet lanes and rotting wharves.

Even before the century of their exodus elapsed, Nantucket's major industry was charm. Steamships brought wealthy off-islanders to the enchanted relic. They lodged at guest houses, built Shingle Style or Colonial Revival houses on Cliff Road, and adopted the fishermen's shanties at Siasconset, the island's outermost end. Meanwhile the winter Nantucketers lived marginally, fishing, farming, or tending the summer people. So Nantucket snoozed into the twentieth century.

The charms of seaside Stonington, Connecticut, endure to delight summer visitors, but the remnants of its salty past are gone.

The handsome houses of Nantucket's Main Street, built or adapted for early-nineteenth-century merchants, still lend the gracious air seen in this 1940s photograph.

After World War II, the town awoke. Tourism quickened: more lumbering ferryboats, more day-trippers, and more and bigger buses on the narrow streets. The sound of motorcycles pierced the quiet air; the motor vehicles proliferated. Crowds eroded the somnolent elegance of the town. Dormancy would not do. "Nantucket had to decide whether it was going to let tourism destroy the very character that brought tourists there in the first place," recalls Walter Beinecke, the man who, above all others, would make that decision. A longtime summer resident of Siasconset and heir to a fortune built on Green Stamps, Beinecke felt he had no choice. So did other Nantucket devotees. In 1955, they created a historic district, the first in New England. The legislation was revolutionary. More to the point, it provided some protection by preventing demolition or alteration of the historic buildings within the densest part of town and at Siasconset. That was just a beginning. "What was still needed," Beinecke later told Nantucket Preservation Institute students, "was the ability to manage tourism for the benefit of the island: proper facilities to meet the needs of tourists without introducing a jarring element." Fiercely loyal to the island's appeal, Beinecke set out to build such facilities. In so doing, he retooled Nantucket in his own image. For decades, the zealous millionaire bought up parcel after parcel of land along the town's historic wharves. Lots covered with unsightly coal and oil structures shed their skins. Beinecke began to engineer a metamorphosis.

Beinecke's stamp was everywhere. It was on Straight Wharf, his major project, with its quick-turnaround ferry-landing and marina, its restaurants and shops, where traditional waterfront shapes and materials cloaked phone booths, water and sewer hookups, and bike racks. It was on the boat basin, where rows of mahogany-trimmed sport-fishing boats from Connecticut and Delaware, and sloops,

ketches, and schooners from Newport, Marblehead, and the Grand Caymans tied up at tidy gray docks. And it was on the piers where shingled art galleries flanked neat, densely packed cottages. While the artful redos drew off-islanders, Nantucketers grew wary. The cute began to cloy. The NO MAN IS AN ISLAND buttons began to dot their lapels, questioning Beinecke control. Was this prettification and tourist-packaging good for Nantucket? Should one man's taste, his artifice, define a whole town? And did this new-old amalgam work?

The Harbor House hotel, a cluster of "Nantucket townhouses" on the outskirts of town, distills these pervasive questions. Like other Beinecke projects, the 111-unit complex of trim buildings softened with weathered shingles, plantings, and curving paths reproduces the intimacy of times and streets past. Unquestionably, these simple renditions surpass the garish architectural growths that scar so much of Cape Cod. But do they create a timeless place or only a coy reminder? Is Nantucket new? Is it old? Who knows? The island has become the built embodiment of a fantasy: Nantucket as the Platonic ideal of a New England whaling village; Nantucket peopled by a new race, an alien—and, to some, disturbing—culture dedicated to pleasure.

In this idyllic setting, controversy still simmers: has Beinecke saved the town or ruined it? The NO MAN IS AN ISLAND buttons are gone but the issues linger.

Not that Beinecke is the only force at work here. The preservation commission he helped launch wields power, too, so much so that Beinecke has found himself in conflict with its conservative cast. Force met force most vividly when the strong-minded developer engaged the commission in a lengthy legal battle on that very Harbor House. A single design detail of the complex began the fight: the roof color for the cluster of houses. Beinecke, who thought a true Nantucket lay in a mix of tones,

One of the oldest houses on Nantucket, this Siasconset fisherman's shack, dated 1675 and bearing the name Auld Lang Syne, typifies the weatherbeaten charm sought after in such reconstructions as the new wharves, top. Though harmonious with the past, their false timelessness has raised criticism.

Classics in contemporary architecture, these twin beach houses, designed by Venturi, Rauch and Scott Brown, blend old and new with their shingles, lunette window, and other off-angle but accommodating elements.

wanted to vary individual units, using three of the approved shades for roof shingles. The commission wanted one harmonious look. Beinecke lost. The monochrome roof won.

Critics of Beinecke, of the commission, and of the Nantucket they have built come in many gradations, too. Purists of one stripe worry about the proscription on modern design. With the district expanded to take in the whole island, they fear the conformity that the controls demand. They look at Venturi, Rauch and Scott Brown's beach houses standing on the dunes outside town. The shingled twosome proves that contemporary innovation and Nantucket tradition can coexist; the structures have won an honor award from the American Institute of Architecture. Would the architects' original yet contextual play with the past be allowed today?

Purists of another stripe look askance at the pseudohistorical shingle tacked to the front of houses originally sheathed in elegant clapboard. Fans of the modern and students of the past alike disparage the inflated 1980s classicism of the summer extravaganzas sprawling across the tight little island. Others wonder about the overall ambience of the island and its conspicuous consumption. "The original home of the $1.50 ice cream cone," caustic critics landmarked the town. Listen closely to the sounds of a summer night on the new Nantucket, wrote the *New York Times*'s Russell Baker, a longtime resident. "It is the sound of the island eating money."

And so, while the crowds come, the debate goes on: Is the real Nantucket being destroyed to save it? As "quainting" and gentrification come to other coastal towns, the question resounds.

Boston by the Sea

Boston, too, is a city with the sea at its front door and a cycle of life and death and rebirth in the history of its harbor. Boston's waterfront life, unlike Nantucket's, lingered into the twentieth century; but as maritime technology changed, its more intrusive ele-

The homely allure of this fishing shack still survives at Edgartown, Martha's Vineyard, Nantucket's sister island.

Fishing boats at Boston's Commercial Wharf and T Wharf: the first revitalized, the other torn down in the 1960s.

ments split the city from the sea. Bulk shipments of grain, wool, coal, and, later, oil demanded larger structures, bigger ships, ever more cavernous warehouses, and the web of rails to serve them. The sense of the sea no longer permeated the city. By 1900, the waterfront where Edward Everett Hale and his boyhood chums had escaped from their studies for an hour or two to watch the "Spanish sailors with bearded lips" and drink in the exotic smells of coffee beans, spices, and hides had vanished into memory. There were two Bostons: a swath of steel rails, pavement, and heavy machinery on a mechanized waterfront, and businesslike downtown, an impenetrable few blocks away. To go to the water, Bostonians left Boston; they journeyed to Nahant, or Hull, or points beyond.

Yet even that waterfront of work was obsolete by the mid-twentieth century. As another generation brought supertankers to pump their volatile contents into tanks and giant cranes to hoist containerized cargoes from ship to truck, the active waterfront moved to roomier outlying parts of the harbor. By the late 1950s, Boston's old downtown waterfront lay derelict: workplace for a languishing industry, home to the hardiest souls, haunt of a scant few salt-seeking walkers.

Still, the eternal lure of waterside life remained. By the early sixties, a few adventurers had opted to carve the vacant warehouses into living quarters by the sea, and some architects began to see the appeal of its architecture and ambience. "Those were

Faneuil Hall Marketplace a hundred years ago, when it was a wholesale market.

rough-and-tumble times down there," architect Tim Anderson recalls. "There was an after-hours bar on Commercial Street, noisy refrigerator trucks with their motors running all night. It was a lot more colorful than now." Anderson and others saw potential. "I figured if people could walk to work, come home and put a sweater on, and go sailing, they'd rent," he says. By 1968, the success of his gutted and remodeled Prince Building proved him right. So did the influx of seaside pioneers that followed. Drawn by the twin appeals of price and place, they filled the loft apartments in the idling wharves.

Public agencies as well as private water-lovers surveyed the shoreline. In 1964, the Boston Redevelopment Authority published a waterfront-renewal plan. In typical sixties style, they neglected its ocean origins: they designed a forest of towers and a moat of roads that cut off the sea, and massive demolition that ousted small businesses for superscale apartments and garages. The public protested. Mass meetings, professional studies, political pressure followed. For two fiery decades, Boston struggled to renew its waterfront.

Central to this struggle—and key to its commercial success—was Faneuil Hall Market. The conversion of the outmoded 1826 market into what became the quintessential symbol of waterfront revitalization in Boston and the United States started slowly. Known to Bostonians as Quincy Market for its early-nineteenth-century sponsor, Mayor Josiah Quincy,

The nineteenth-century columns of Alexander Parris's Quincy Market now preside over a new age of food purveyors in an interior design by Benjamin Thompson Associates.

WATERFRONTS: DOWN TO THE SEASHORE AND RIVERSIDE 67

this massive domed and Greek-columned granite market hall flanked by matching brick and granite commercial buildings looked lost when its meat-and-produce-distribution days ended.

Today, when Faneuil Hall Marketplace boasts a legendary sales volume per square foot, and more visitors some years than Disney World, it is hard to remember how close it came to rubble. Still, it took a decade of debate to establish the market's right to a future. Eventually, the city secured nearly $10 million in urban-renewal funds to buy out leases, relocate tenants, and install utilities. Some $2.3 million in HUD historic-preservation funds restored the hand-

some granite façades and slate roofs to their 1826 appearance. Still, no bank would venture funds to turn it into an urban shopping mall. "Everybody knew it would fail," says developer James Rouse. Visionary enough to suspect otherwise, Rouse finally secured $30 million from a consortium of lenders. In 1976, 150 years to the day after its dedication, he opened the first of three buildings. In the first year of operation, ten million visitors testified to his vision. "Boston created a lot of believers," says Rouse. Since then, mini-marketplaces across the country have confirmed their faith. "That experience lit a lot of fires around the country," the developer observes. It "lit fires" in Boston, too. As tourists and shoppers spilled forth, they added to the development of an ever-widening ring around the markets—out along State Street, and down to the harbor once again.

Today, the waterfront has become the Waterfront, lively, still colorful, but pricey and rather precious. Great granite warehouses once filled with bales of cotton and wool serve quiche and chowder amid a forest of ferns; wharves where dockworkers heaved chests of tea and silk from the holds of China clippers house designer-jean-clad condominium owners.

Such upscale success upsets many. Seaside chic, say critics, threatens the real life of the sea, sweeping away fishermen, lobstermen, ferry riders, Sunday sailors, and even walkers in its wake. The forbidding designs of new buildings say "keep out" to strollers, joggers, and others seeking public access to the open space of the sea along the two-mile stretch of waterfront from Charlestown to South Boston. The cost and scarcity of dock space caused the Boston Educational and Marine Association to declare it "the most

Today's fishermen have scant space amidst the brick beauties of Boston's old wharves. Here, the salad-bar style of the Chart House.

Where China clippers and fishing boats once docked, pleasure craft and condominiums now sit on Commercial Wharf.

inhospitable port in America." Would a city in desperate financial straits and dependent on the property tax for income encourage the development that destroyed the harbor? asks Thom Ennen, head of Boston Harbor Associates. "I like to tell people that if Noah had built the ark the way Boston has built the waterfront, we'd all have gills," he says.

By the 1980s, Boston's waterfront had attracted enough projects to concern a growing constituency who foresaw the death of its water-based life. They cast a wary eye on the gargantuan developments edging out to the south; they protested against plans for mega-structures spilling from the old waterfront to the turn-of-the-century Fort Point Channel enclave. Here, where the Boston Wharf Company's massive brick warehouses for wool and fruit brood over the narrow bridge-spanned channel, where the grandiose Commonwealth Pier of 1912 dominates a vast cleared area—here in a two-mile stretch this decade's waterfront battle rages. Waterfront revitalization for whom? Not for the fishermen who have docked here for decades; nor, for that matter, for the artists who pioneered lofts here. Museums, marinas, offices, condominiums, and restaurants squeeze them both. "Look around," says lobsterman Archie Morell, surveying the "musical piers" with dismay. "There isn't a spot for a lobster boat from here to Atlantic Avenue." And still City Hall holds plans and models for multi-million-dollar complexes.

To the north, across the Charles River, rehabilitation proceeds in a more orderly way. Here, the Charlestown Navy Yard, closed down by the Navy in 1974 after nearly two centuries, has evolved into one of the more ambitious reuse projects in the country.

Unlike most upscaled structures, the granite Mercantile Wharf Buildings, made over by architect John Sharratt for the Massachusetts Housing and Finance Agency, house residents with mixed incomes.

Blending with both the scale of the Fort Point Channel area and the trusses of its old bridge, this building by Notter Finegold and Alexander honors the context of Boston's changing waterfront.

Blessed with fine buildings to supply context and compelled by the Monuments Transfer Act of 1974 to plan cooperatively, the city and the National Park Service have begun to transform a hundred acres of prime waterfront land and dozens of historic military and industrial buildings into a truly water-based community.

From the dock in front of the factory-turned-apartment-building, Boston's shoreline renaissance is salty and sometimes splendid. Beyond the new parks, past the World War II destroyer USS *Cassin Young* and its elder, the frigate USS *Constitution,* the downtown skyline rises across the boat-filled harbor. Like old lithographs of the clipper-ship city, the scenario

Vacant for years, the Charlestown Navy Yard holds condominiums as part of a public-private plan.

is striking evidence that Bostonians have come home to their waterfront.

But questions remain: What kind of waterfront will it be? Will the downtown real-estate dogma of "highest and best use," of private property above all, reign here too? Or will the old Puritan-based tradition of "ways to the water" guarantee public access? And what of the harbor itself—Boston's front yard? What of its polluted waters and long-neglected islands? Can the public overcome the pollution and the misuse and ward off the assaults of private profiteers to make the harbor a public playground and public transportation link again? Above all, can the harbor handle the business of the sea along with the enjoyment of it? In the midst of boom, the struggle for Boston's waterfront has just begun.

Portsmouth: A Peninsula That Found Itself

By contrast, Portsmouth, New Hampshire, is a waterfront that never cut itself off from the sea. Turn anywhere in this handsome old city and water surrounds you. Downtown Portsmouth sits on a ragged peninsula at the mouth of the Piscataqua River; ocean, river, and tidal estuary cut into the coastline to create a distinct waterfront on every side, a seabound ring bringing life to downtown. Surrounding and penetrating the historic district centered on Market Square, the ocean flavors Portsmouth's renaissance. For all the trendy brick planters and food stands, it is an easy, rough-edged restoration. Somehow, Portsmouth's salty past of shipbuilding and

fishing cohabits with its present of Izods and Topsiders.

How has the town kept this sense of identity, yet survived? Credit geography, history, and economics. Geography gave Portsmouth its diverse waterfronts; geography and history combined to preserve them. Elsewhere, late-nineteenth-century waterfronts expanded and renewed themselves at the expense of their earlier character; industrial-scale structures replaced the old human-scale ones. Portsmouth's didn't. It simply grew upriver, leaving the old waterfront shabby but intact. The gradual decline of Portsmouth's shipping preserved the scale of the downtown waterfront, while the Navy Yard across the river in Kittery kept, and still keeps, the maritime heritage alive. To this day, the ship-studded Navy Yard and the State Pier upriver anchor the restoration of the Portsmouth waterfront in reality. Against this backdrop, even the museum works; the re-created gundalow tied up at Prescott Park and the submarine recently installed upriver amplify a heritage rather than fabricate a sentimental reminder of one.

On a summer day, Richard Candee, a preservation consultant here, surveys the scene from an outdoor cafe and considers why Portsmouth seems so at ease. Revitalization came from individuals, he says, and it came late. No self-conscious single master plan, funded and philosophized from on high, slotted the city into some mono-minded Quincy Market or Newburyport. "By the time Portsmouth began its restoration," Candee notes, "preservationists knew more about what worked and what didn't." Their piecemeal, small-scale maneuvers allowed individual interpretation, individual financing, individual results. That is, after all, how most towns evolved in the first

Signs of work at sea enliven the Portsmouth waterfront as seen from Ceres Street.

place. "Of course," Candee goes on, scanning a modern plate-glass window marring a Federal-era façade, "it's far from perfect." In this case, the Historic District Commission lacked the power to review the windows, a "minor" detail with a major impact on the look of the buildings. Today's sensibility will trade off sterile historicism for "reality."

In some places larger ills than tasteless window treatment assault Portsmouth's landscape, too; glaring gaps caused by insensitive urban renewal before the district was established scar the city. Even Portsmouth's Strawbery Banke, a museum village, tore down the Victorian houses on its site. Nonetheless, without such destruction, Portsmouth might never have rallied to save itself. "You usually need losses like that before you can get a district," Candee observes.

No district can cope with other urban issues. Poverty persists. Asphalt shingles still camouflage eighteenth- and nineteenth-century houses. Underuse and underfinancing cloud the future of even such historic gems as the eighteenth-century Wentworth-Gardner house. Conversely, prosperity from the sprawl of industry in the southern tier of New Hampshire troubles the city. "Gentrification" has entered the Portsmouth vernacular, too. South Enders worry that high-priced condominiums will force them out. Meanwhile, insensitive public agencies like the state highway department still attack Portsmouth's landscape: their mountain of highway salt isolates the State Pier from the rest of the waterfront, while a monster bridge threatens to overwhelm the fishing village near South Mill Pond.

Finally, out in the harbor, one more enigma looms: the old Portsmouth Naval Prison, a gloomy yet compelling giant, broods over its island and dominates the ocean view. A landmark, now vacant, its fate is unsure; how do you recycle a prison beside a military installation and not compromise security? Persistent problems. Hard questions. But fifty years ago, or even twenty-five, the question about Portsmouth was more difficult to solve: how do you revive a seafaring town, past its prime and mired in poverty? Today, Portsmouth has answered that question by making its maritime heritage the lynchpin of revitalization.

Portland's Sense of the Sea

Further up the coast—or "down" in Yankee terms—Portland's waterfront also retains its sense of the sea. A decade behind Portsmouth or Boston in terms of upscale amenities, the waterside of the Maine city hungers for a bit of seaside chic. Yet its rough ocean air is appealing. For all its past poverty, Portland's

Portland at the turn of the century: some of these workaday signs of the city still endure amidst the accouterments of twentieth-century tourism.

waterfront still means business. From the massive steel-framed structures of the Bath Iron Works to the giant cranes of the Portland Ship Repair Facility, signs of working life loom large. The railroad tracks running down the center of Commercial Street are shiny from use. The Nova Scotia ferry terminal near the bridge to South Portland still serves passengers daily. Side by side, on both sides of Commercial Street, remnants of yesterday's waterfront have made peace with today's. Great brick warehouses with gutsy rusticated granite post-and-lintel bases hold their own among the modern structures. Visually and economically, they mesh with surprising ease in the midst of refurbishment.

Some of these buildings purvey upscale wares: Food Works flourishes its yellow awning; Dimillo's Floating Restaurant, anchored streetside, displays a sailor figurine and coy nautical signage. Others carry on old waterfront ways: Carr Ship Chandlery and Jordan Wholesale Meats endure. The Rufus Deering Lumber sign still proclaims FOUNDED 1830 in gilt on its gemlike office. Between Bath Iron Works and the coming $15 million fish pier and industrial buildings

to the east, the almost-three-mile harbor is a salty site, a place of unkempt edges.

Up the hill, however, the balance shifts. At the Old Port Exchange, the boutiquing begins. The small shops and bricked streets leading up from the sea are Portland's formal preservation "victory." Wrought on the theme of fine crafts and *haute cuisine*, they teem with tourist life and boast adaptive reuse—shoe factory to gallery, armory to hotel. Built after the Great Fire of 1866, the buildings along Exchange and Market streets could serve as a textbook of Victorian eclecticism: brick, sandstone, cast iron, and granite; Italianate, French, and Romanesque designs. Shops with names like the Chocolate Soldier and the Paper Patch flag down visitors. But their corollaries—the banished hardware store, the bygone printer—distress some. Many who find the Exchange the epitome of a success story from an economic standpoint deplore its conservation failures—the seventies-style sandblasting that eroded brick surfaces, the destructive masonry work, the remodeling that thrust mock-historic storefronts onto authentic Victorian structures. And yet, for all such flaws, Exchange Street is a pedestrian pleasureground, and Portland has remained Portland. It has resisted the twin-pronged attacks of poverty and prosperity. The demolition of the seventies was stayed, on the one hand, and the *nouvelle* niceties that could have smothered the life out of the city's waterfront have not.

Will it stay that way? "People are afraid what's happened to Boston will happen to Portland's waterfront," historian Arthur Gerrier responds, eyeing the waterfront's first residential housing in seven years, a 150-year-old warehouse turned into twenty-four condominiums. Meanwhile, architects and developers counter that the public still has no access to the sight of the sea. Private fish piers preclude picnics.

Fishermen resist the amenities that attract the public. Can sushi bars and fish factories coexist? Can the work of the sea and the play that refreshes coexist?

Joel Russ, preservationist and planner turned real-estate consultant, the transformer of that warehouse to condominiums, thinks so. A former director of Greater Portland Landmarks, Russ believes that "there is a demand for both kinds of activities on almost all waterfronts" and that Portland can accommodate both maritime enterprises and recreational ones. He insists that workers and pleasure-seekers can have equal access to the ocean. Portland has encouraged the conflicting parties to engage in a dialogue to ensure this, Russ says. A 1973 "City Edges" study funded by the National Endowment for the Arts started the conversation. A decade later, city zoning codified it, allotting space to economic activities that depend on the water plus more tourist-oriented ones. "That's the balance that the city and the developers are going to have to see through," says Russ. Gentrification may not tilt Portland's balance. With design guidelines to promote quality architecture and with a fishing business sturdy enough to remain viable, Portland's harbor could stay seaworthy.

From Eastport to Block Island, the same need for balance characterizes many of New England's seaside sites. As the region returns to the water, those who love it must think of these animated edges as both a public room with a view and a working place. Guardians of New England must struggle to protect both the pleasure-seeking present and the working life that has defined New England's waterfront history and will ensure its future vitality.

Within paces of the old seaport lies the clutch of shops that bring tourist life to the Old Port Exchange.

*Engineers pose at the Merrimack Canal, a part of the
great enterprise built to power the mills in Lowell,
Massachusetts.*

4. Mills and Milltowns: Where Life Meets Work

"In Massachusetts, every fall in the rivers of the second class, such as the Merrimack and the Charles, and indeed, every 'privilege' upon the smallest and most insignificant streams, has been seized upon for the use of small farms or factories," the Hadley Falls Company reported in 1853. So it was. So it remains. Veined with waterways, New England had numberless sites for its mills and factories. Rivers of great heft and small streams licking rocky beds, rapids with steep drops and river paths with shallow runs fueled the industrial revolution.

"You can almost say 'How many towns are there in New England?' and then multiply by one and a half and say 'That's how many mills,'" says Frank Beard of the Maine Historical Commission. The tight-knit complex of mill-towns spilling and settling around the mills reflected the integration of work and life—an architecture to

Massed in muscular simplicity and punctuated by its characteristic stair towers, the mill complex on the Lamprey River in New Market, New Hampshire, stands as a striking symbol of this dominant New England architecture.

serve the people who served the wheels. The first cotton mill, the Slater Mill in Pawtucket, Rhode Island, founded in 1793, became a prototype: a village with two tenements for workers, a grander home for the owner, and a company store. But it was Lowell that established the image. The first and most fully planned industrial town, the Spindle City on the Merrimack set the course in 1822 with 5.6 miles of canals and chains of buildings—mills, stores, factory housing, churches, and mansions. Though its workers changed from Yankee to immigrant as New England changed, and its power changed from water to steam, the legacy of the mill as a total web of life—a planned community and distinctive social organization—persisted.

"What a seat of wealth . . . focus of activity . . . nursery of invention," a nineteenth-century booster wrote. Symbolically enough, a beehive, the emblem of

Asphalt shingles can't obscure the appeal of factory housing in Palmer, Massachusetts, part of the total mill complex of buildings for life and work.

buzzing labor, became the insignia for the mill city Holyoke.

Framing new notions of space, time, and work, the mill's buildings inevitably shaped a new form of architecture. "The modern parent and the first born of modern building technology," historian James Marston Fitch has called it. Whether massed in the muscular simplicity of masonry or lined crisply in wood, punctuated by bell tower or turret, the mill was sited with an eye to the fall of water and the slope of land that made it work. Elegant dams—engineering feats in their day—and elaborate canals channeled the water's energy to ever larger complexes of mill buildings. Yankee ingenuity at its finest, the mill, melded to the rushing water that powered it, made and still makes a commanding presence on the New England landscape. "The planning—or the best of it—largely survives," notes John Coolidge, author of the classic *Mill and Mansion.* "The main street, parallel to the river, lined with public and semi-public buildings, the areas set aside for parks, and the orderly lineup of the corporation's buildings" endure. So, he suggests, does the "sense of community" and identity that made Manchester, Lowell, and Holyoke self-conscious to a degree beyond their peer cities and blessed them with an array of fine architecture to this day.

Certainly not every mill was a glorious down-by-the-old-millstream structure. Often, a legion of additions, some adroit, some ramshackle, crowded around. The tall chimneys of the steam-generators later blackened the sky. Above all, life for the men, women, and children at the loom was cruel and harsh and often devoid of amenities. Though these were not England's "dark satanic mills," existence at the low end of America's industrial ladder was never idyllic. "It was only a wonder that life can dwell in such apartments," said a report on Holyoke in 1872. Mill and milltown, the architectural embodiment of an exploitative way of life, earned scant love.

Nonetheless, the mill was central to New England's economic and social existence in the nineteenth and early twentieth centuries. As late as 1900, Massachusetts, the key industrial state of the region, led the nation in making boots, shoes, and textiles; it was fourth only to the much larger states of New York, Pennsylvania, and Illinois in total industrial output.

That productivity didn't last. In the twentieth century, competition from the South, with its raw materials, cost-cutting labor, and new plants (often financed by New Englanders) doomed the Northern mills. As the shoe and textile industries declined, their slide carried New England's economy with it. The empty mills symbolized the drift. The word *milltown* became synonymous with *ghost town*. Before mid-century, mills were shabby collections of blank-eyed buildings, surly enclaves depressing the towns and workers around them. FOR SALE OR LEASE said the signs across the boarded windows. MILLS ARE A KURSE, says a graffiti writer's scrawl that still lingers on a mill building in Lawrence, Massachusetts. "Sociological curiosities," Coolidge's *Mill and Mansion* described them more dispassionately in 1942. "Their architecture is always ignored," he observed. "Yet, natural though this neglect is, it is not deserved." Poet Albert T. Klyberg summed up the scene:

Turret-towered textile towns
silhouetted in silent valleys.
Tattered tares, withered fruit of the loom flutter
faded, frayed; hanging limp
in gnarled orchards of muted machines.

Made-Over Mills

Fortunately Coolidge's words, not the bleak poem of the period, forecast the future of these empty shells. Barely a generation later, a conference on mill buildings could register more pragmatists than pre-

Almost two centuries old, Slater Mill in Pawtucket, Rhode Island, the first urban mill complex, now houses a museum showing the way New England's textile industry began.

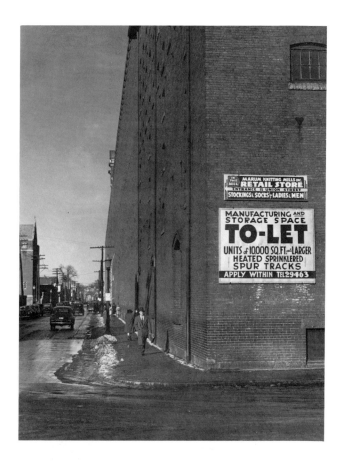

TO-LET, but no lessees responded to the downtrodden Lawrence mills, captured by Farm Service Administration photographer Jack Delano in 1941.

to Ralph Lauren discounts in Lawrence's Everett Mills. All told, more than fifty New England mills have been converted into apartments, according to one estimate, and even more have been made into offices.

For every history-packed Slater Mill Museum in Pawtucket that traces the mill past, there are a hundred mills that now contain the present. Sold at $2 a square foot as lofts or sliced into slick $50-a-square-foot spaces complete with butcher block and broadloom, the renovated mill has become almost a cliché. Its adaptive use has become so commonplace that *Yankee* magazine thought it a novelty to run an article on a mill recycled into (of all things) a mill. Many New Englanders now see the mill as more shell than historic structure. Michael Folsom, who switched from teaching literature at MIT to running the Charles River Museum of Industry at Waltham, recalls a cocktail-party chat with a developer of mills. "Like Molière's Bourgeois Gentilhomme, who was delighted to learn he was speaking prose, this guy was delighted to know he was a preservationist," says Folsom. The 1814 mill complex where Folsom's museum is located holds a harpsichord factory, housing for the elderly, artists' studios, and shops.

After a generation's hiatus, even the people in the milltowns have begun to look objectively at their architectural pariahs. "No one in Peabody, Massachusetts, will ever want to live in those buildings! They remember too much about them," critics of a plan to turn the town's old tannery into housing for the elderly scoffed in the 1970s. By the 1980s, the project was filled.

Such a swing is not sudden. The revolution was two decades in the making. Here and there, as early as the 1960s, some mills had already begun to find a few tenants and to serve as cheap space for an innovative offshoot of the textile business: the mill outlet, with its pipe racks and spartan mill interior, gave birth to

servationists. The mill owners assembled in 1983 were calling themselves "developers," and their operating assumption was that mills are desirable, that they are "developable," that the future is theirs. Clearly, something had happened. Only a decade before, the same owners had read an Arthur D. Little study telling them there was "nothing of aesthetic or economic value" in the mills, recalls Laurence Gross, curator for industrial technology at the Museum of American Textile History. Now they saw a thriving market for their property. "What's a New England growth industry for the late 1980s?" *New England Business* asked in July 1983. "Mills—nineteenth-century mills," it answered. Mills now hold everything from microplastics in Clinton, Massachusetts, to Helikon Furniture in Norwich, Connecticut; from an arts enterprise in New Hampshire's Belknap Mills

After a fire and abandonment, this textile mill in Clinton, Massachusetts, was retooled into low- and middle-income housing by the Architects Collaborative.

the discount store. By the late sixties and seventies, the mill was attracting and incubating a second sort of entrepreneur, the technological pioneers who founded Wang, DEC, and the countless smaller high-technology companies spinning off from Route 128 around Boston. Finding cheap rents and flexible space in the empty industrial attics of New England, they made the mill an asset, first in the parts of New England most pressed for space, and finally in the distant corners of the region. Somehow, it seemed, the entrepreneurial spirit that made the mills in the first place had found a home in them again.

What galvanized this mill revival? Was it only cheap rents and easy electric and sewer hookups? Was it the Tax Act of 1981, with its 25 percent tax credit for rehabilitating historic structures? Was it a ready work force or the vagaries of fashion? Or was it because these old buildings are ultimately adaptable, better built, and endowed with a greater sense of place than their antiseptic heirs?

However one assesses all these factors, the success is real and spills into its surroundings. In the twentieth as in the nineteenth century, New England's mills and milltowns are kin. The condition of the mill both reflects and causes the condition of the surrounding village or city: as the mills go, so go their towns.

Manchester's Amoskeag Mills

The main street of Manchester, New Hampshire, still wears the legacy of old attitudes. The grim roadway that passes the Amoskeag mills is symbolic: a franchise-dominated, asphalt-encased wasteland, it mirrors the neglect to the historic mill complex along its path. The ultimate mill city in its dramatic conception, Manchester is also an archetype in its decline. Today, it is hard to believe that, beginning in

The graceful sweep of Amoskeag's lower canal building and mill tower, shot by would-be rescuer Randolph Langenbach in 1968. Four years later the redevelopment agency hardtopped the waters and tore down major pieces of this Manchester, New Hampshire, mill.

1838, more than a hundred mills, summoned into being by the fifty-foot drop of the Merrimack River, were powered by a milldam. Built by the same entrepreneurs who created Lowell, Manchester was the world's largest textile plant, "a walled medieval city," laced by canals. The bell tower embodying a "sense of pride," the buildings of matching brick, the congenial corporate housing, all contributed to the ambience, Randolph Langenbach writes in *Amoskeag: Life and Work in an American Factory-City.*

A hundred years later that ambience was doomed. "As Lowell represented the first impact of the Industrial Revolution on the [Merrimack] valley, Manchester embodied its full development and, the next century, its catastrophic collapse," historian Joseph Thorndike observed. The attrition of the mills was hastened by their very dominance. "Here was this large core of buildings, this center of the city that was no longer a viable or useful thing. And enormous," Elizabeth Lessard of the Manchester Historic Association remembers. The mentality of the auto age speeded their collapse. In 1972, the canal's border of buildings was flattened for a highway; its waterways were drained and hardtopped. To some, it was the most philistine attack of the down-with-the-mills era. "In terms of floor space, only fifteen or twenty percent was lost," says Langenbach, but "in terms of the quality of the urban design, they came close to leveling one hundred percent."

Today, the remains reinforce his words. They create a dreary reminder of that age of indifference. And yet, even here, the eighties have brought a change in attitude from city planners and the larger population. Inspired by Langenbach's *Amoskeag* exhibition at Manchester's Currier Gallery in 1975 and by mill revival everywhere, attitudes have shifted. "There's been a big change," says developer John C. Madden. Some manufacturers survived the exodus; Pandora knitwear stayed nearby and moved into refurbished space. High-technology companies joined them. So did Velcro—half space-age firm, half mill. Madden himself recently made over 200,000 square feet of the Manchester Mills. "A total variety," he describes the blend of new-age and old-style tenants. "It's good space, it's flexible, it's conveniently located. These buildings have got a lot of life in them." The tragedy is that so much of Amoskeag vanished before the resurrection.

Lowell's Hildreth Building, seen in its 1890s state of grace, fell victim to declining days, then saw rebirth once more in the fixup sparked by its designation as a national park.

Birth and Rebirth at Lowell

While Manchester stands as a symbol of twentieth-century desecration, Lowell, its nineteenth-century parent, survived to become a symbol of another sort. To display what it labeled "the most important planned industrial city in America," the National Park Service created a historic monument out of the entire city. The phrase is printed in a brochure that carries the buffalo stamp of the U.S. Department of the Interior. Equally, the revival bears the imprint of a constituency that cared. Unlike Manchester, this city kindled native pride; it inspired zealots on behalf of its downtrodden mills. Patrick Mogan, a school superintendent with a passion for the past, was the first in a list of Lowell crusaders. Before they finished, the state had begun its $15 million investment program in 1977 and Lowell-born Congressman Paul Tsongas had engineered the federal legislation creating the park in 1978.

Here, where the falls of the Merrimack once powered a model milltown of world renown, Lowell joined the National Park Service to create a model of another sort. Not an isolated hothouse, not a re-creation of one static moment in American history, the park is the city. Winding through the downtown, it encompasses mill and main street, canal and mansion. The park is not only a living museum, but a place of ongoing life.

Lowell fit the framework for a unique milltown exhibit. Because this "Eldorado on the Merrimack" was first to harness a complete environment to the machine, it earned early architectural applause. Because it brought a total workforce to a site on a larger scale than before, it embodied the social impact of New England's industrial revolution. And, because it held the quilt of ethnic groups that came to turn the wheels of other spindle cities of the century, it exem-

The light-filled atrium designed by Perry, Dean, Rogers and Partners creates a vibrant entrance within the low-key Wannalancit Mill.

plified the "Other American Revolution." This "City of Nations," where a millowner might send out announcements to workers in eleven languages, still stands as an emblem of America, and so the Lowell park exhibits it: not only as an architectural and industrial enterprise but also as a city of many ethnic groups, enduring over time.

Equally important, Lowell's planners aimed to revive the whole downtown, to use historic preservation to improve the quality of life. And so they have. "All of a sudden Lowell went from the most unemployment to the least," says architect Simeon Bruner, an early planner. Around the park, an ungainly mix of city, state, federal, and private agencies began to revitalize the dreary milltown. Spurred to a near-miracle of cooperation by the presence of the park and the push of Congressman Tsongas, private and public officials spearheaded the revival of storefronts, the recycling of mills into housing for the elderly, low-income housing, and workspace, plus the fixup of streets and sidewalks. "Ten years ago, everyone thought the national park was a delusion," Fred Faust, director of the Lowell Historic Commission for much of the period, recalls. A decade and $115 million in public investment and loans, combined with the computer boom brought by Wang and others, changed that prediction, and Lowell itself.

By the mid-eighties, some seventy-eight buildings had a new life. "Take your place in history," one mill advertised space for rent, capitalizing on a once-scorned heritage. Other mills had become models of the recycler's art. Strikingly, the Wannalancit Mill not only boasts a splendid interior but stands as a paradigm of public-private cooperation. After months of maneuvering with the owners, the Park

Plagued by two major fires and on the way to ruin, the Lowell Manufacturing Company became part of the park's visitor center, today called the Market Mills.

Service swapped land nearby for a parking lot in exchange for exhibition space within the mill. Such cooperation means that the linear walkway passing by the Wannalancit will connect the park's headquarters, the boat rides, and the trolley with the recycled mill itself.

Not all the new projects work so well. The Lower Lock Complex, refurbished with $2 million in park amenities, holds a $24 million, 250-room Hilton, a banal brick building designed by Skidmore, Owings, and Merrill. Alas, this awkward architectural ensemble sits on the most prominent site in the city. Nonetheless, for every ugly incursion in the streetscape—a bank that pushes a driveway through a corner sidewalk or the grim façades of fast-food or franchise shops—a dozen insertions either fit in the context or better it. Design review and control have also called a halt to the defacing of old buildings with gaudy signs. Combined with community consciousness, they set standards for incoming companies. "We haven't had buildings lost," says Faust. "Things have been done very sensitively."

Today, this depressed mill city has turned around. Though nine hundred buildings remain ripe for rehabilitation, the mills have stabilized. Those not filled with computer companies no longer seem likely to be lost to fire as before, one a year. Work to restore or simply repair historic buildings goes on and accounts for some of the five thousand jobs created in the city since the park was formed. With it all, Lowell remains a living city: a downtown window is as likely to display plastic flowers as hand-dipped candles. As Faust puts it: "We have rough edges, but we're real."

Wannalancit developers Dobreth and Fryer also kept the spectacular staircase in the recycled mill. Where millworkers once moved between floors of looms, high-tech office workers walk now.

Somehow, the first inspiration of the Lowell superintendent of schools endures: volumes of plans and bureaucratic input have not stultified the city. Reagan-era cutbacks and curtailments have not stopped the momentum. Community beginnings—local supporters coached by their politicians—launched the Lowell revival and still influence it. History and good design have proven themselves to be good business. The Lowell approach has even inspired the state to launch a dozen "mini-Lowells": its Urban Heritage State Parks program received $77 million to use for public and private development in depressed cities throughout the Commonwealth.

Will Lowell "take its place among the gems of our national heritage," as the Park Service hopes? Will visitors from throughout the United States and the world add one more destination—Lowell—to their list of Yellowstone, Yosemite, Gettysburg? Whatever the future of this "second Lowell Experiment," the confluence of countless agencies and individuals, like the confluence of the waterways and machinery that powered this model town, will have major consequences. Lowell remains a sign that America values its urban as well as its natural preserves.

Harrisville's Small-Scale Revival

The rejuvenation of the mills at Harrisville, New Hampshire, is a small-scale project compared to the work at Lowell. Yet, for New England's countless mills and milltowns, it is more of a model. A few hours and a complete mind-set away, this rural mill-town is a success story, too. For, in the years since 1970, Harrisville's mills have made an even longer leap, from the nineteenth century to the twenty-first.

The small town of Harrisville (population, 800) in southwestern New Hampshire looks more like a bucolic college campus dotted with brick buildings than a high-tech hideaway. Clichés like *unspoiled* and *picturesque* come to mind in this enclave where brick mills straddle Goose Brook and small ponds lead one to another in a postcard scene. They will appear on no tourist postcards, however. And the omission is deliberate. "We try never to promote the town," says John ("Chick") Colony, a sixth-generation member of the family that ran the town's woolen mills. No invitations go out from Harrisville. There are no public toilets, no fast or fancy food, no tourist shows. "It is a very special place," says Colony. "There was a great sense that we did not want to ruin the town by saving it."

The canal of Harrisville, New Hampshire, glides past the public library on the left and founder Charles C. P. Harris's house.

Refurbishment of Lewiston's main street with government funds both fuels and derives from the sense of place encouraged by the new use of its old mills.

In the late fifties, ruin-by-exodus, not inundation-by-tourists, was the problem. In 1970, "the mill went out," Colony remembers, and nothing went in. "Town for Sale," was the title of an article in *Yankee* magazine. No matter that the magazine's pages showed a harmonious complex of deep-red mills and masonry walls that went back to 1830. No matter that its citizenry loved it. That was the nadir. "I don't know what it is about the town, but people have always appreciated it," says Colony. Finally, the townspeople arose. Soon they made a "desperate move," in Colony's words. In dire straits, Historic Harrisville incorporated, and, in 1971, raised $50,000 to buy six structures.

In other towns at the time, such labors might have gone to found mill museums, to coax tourists, or to subdivide the floors for industry. Historic Harrisville's Colony was "rash enough" to raise money for "a wild scheme"—something far more holistic and abstract—"an integrated environmental and economic plan for the community." That integration meant securing tenants in both handcrafts and high technology, to be roommates in the buildings overlooking the bucolic stream.

One by one they came: by 1980, the tenth anniversary of Historic Harrisville, the birthday map was dotted with such tenants as weavers and solar-age and computer magazines. Some solar inventors disappeared, undermined by Reagan administration cutbacks in funding for energy research; some of the craftspeople live borderline lives. Nonetheless, "woolen yarn is still being spun in town as it has been in every year since 1790," says Colony. Today, Historic Harrisville's $40,000 budget manages to underwrite an occasional needy tenant, while the paying tenants maintain the historic town.

Low profile, low on heroics, Historic Harrisville hit on the most accommodating kind of preservation: "We've always found that when you make mills into apartments, it's expensive. If you pull in tourists, you lose real life. But when you take a mill and make it have a mill life with small crafts or water-power users, it's not so difficult," Colony insists. "People ask me if I'm in business or preservation. If it weren't for preservation, I wouldn't be in business."

Lewiston: The Nitty-Gritty

No one would call Lewiston, Maine, a hothouse for cutting-edge endeavors like Harrisville or a laboratory for a bureaucratic experiment like Lowell. Nonetheless, the more mundane fixup of its once-bleak mills is further proof that pragmatists as well as preservationists support mill life.

In this corridor of central Maine, the "twin cities"

Beneath the calm of the classic elms, by the tranquil waters of the old canal, life goes on in the Androscoggin Mill of Lewiston, Maine, where a former rayon mill serves as a warehouse.

Some mills endure as mills: also on the Androscoggin River, the oldest building for papermaking in Maine, constructed in 1863, carries on as offices and a paper-converting plant for the Pejetscot paper division of the Hearst Corporation in Topsham.

of Lewiston and Auburn face each other across the dramatic breach of the Androscoggin River—a striking vista in the still gray landscape of Maine's second-most-populated region. Despite the spectacle of the stunning falls, their workhorse days ebbed when the mills emptied out and local industries headed south in the early 1960s. Those of Lewiston's seven mills whose owners didn't flee simply folded, leaving acres of empty floor space and three thousand unemployed workers. Who could possibly fill the echoing rooms of these idle lofts? Who could revive this epitome of a depressed New England milltown?

While the town mourned the moribund mills, a trucking-company owner responded to these questions. Robert A. Roy, who had trucked the waste out of those self-same buildings, bought his first major mill in 1963. Earlier, the energetic Lewiston native had bought a baby version, 30,000 square feet for a scant $6,500 ("less than you need to buy a Honda now," he recalls), and in the days after World War II had roofed and repaired and profited from it. Roy knew, all the same, that filling major space "wasn't easy. The odds were against you." His friends knew it, too. They offered warnings but little else. Still, Roy looked at these structures neither as relics of another day nor as hulks waiting the demolition that hit the Auburn shoe factories across the river. He saw them as space. Space for real estate development. Space to parcel out piecemeal. Buying three mills in a decade, Roy secured tenants for them. By the 1980s, fifty or sixty companies, ranging from cabinetmakers to electronics firms, provided enough diversity to withstand the shock of any single bankruptcy. As a result, Lewiston's mills boast a better-than-90-percent occupancy rate, and to those who feared he'd lose his shirt, Roy replies: "Today, I have to say I have a pretty good shirt on."

The city of Lewiston as a whole has also benefited.

Despite Maine's unemployment and low salary scale, despite gaps where shops fled for three malls nearby, signs of revitalization appear on its six streets. New trees line Main and Lisbon streets, and government-financed façade and street improvements have combined with the mill fixup to help the shabby milltown stitch itself together. "At one time a lot of people thought we were second rate," says city assessor Rodrique Fernand. "I think that Lewiston as a whole is getting away from that."

Setting the Mill to Work

As such structures fill, mill survival itself has gone beyond mere structural salvation. As mills become less of an endangered species, their devotees go beyond caring for their architecture alone: they worry about their identity. How skillful is the reuse? How sensitive the redesign? Others hope to retain mills as industrial entities, not just as structures whose skins cover gutted and slicked-over interiors. The most devoted, historians and archaeologists among them, worry that the mills' historic machinery is vanishing,

Industrial archaeologists among others mourn the removal of the old machinery that showed the way America worked. Here, the Forge Shop in Charlestown, Massachusetts, after its final shutdown.

and with it the presence of the past. At the least, such concern for aesthetics and historical validity shows that the crisis in preserving the mill has passed.

Finally, what of the waters? Despite the original integrity of mill and millstream, the power of the region's rushing waters often remains untapped. In the last decade, however, the energy crisis, and federal laws forcing utility companies to buy their power, have prompted small hydro projects along with rehabilitation. Today, many old mills have made the move to tap the power that roars and trickles across New England. "A large amount of the generating capacity of the Merrimack has been restored," says one such restorer, Gordon Marker, president of the Essex company organized by the founders of Lawrence in 1845. Parallel activity goes on throughout the region. In North Kingston, Rhode Island, two large mills, made into condominiums by architect William Warner, will generate electricity through the original machinery, using the old millrace. Other hydropower plants have appeared in Goodrich Falls, New Hampshire, Winooski, Vermont, and Bangor, Maine. In a region that pays dearly in environmental and financial costs to create or import energy, such projects should multiply. Only then will the mill-preservation picture be complete.

The pictures does fall short of perfection, then. Some milltowns, still lacerated by the end of their economic life, continue to do architectural penance for their poverty. Mills, here and there, may crumble into all-too-picturesque ruins, while others are slicked into a commerce whose only aesthetic attribute is survival. Nonetheless, one feels gratitude for their endurance, and optimism for their renewal. Prophets of a flourishing future and reminders of the days of prosperity left behind, mills have begun to stabilize. Prominent and splendid, they stand as a sign that New England's heritage can be a help to its future.

An open atrium, space-age fixtures, and bold pipes fill this industrial recycling by Blydenburgh Design Development at Davol Square in Providence, Rhode Island.

*The three-decker—multifamily living for much of
New England—now earns respect as an imaginative
historic form of mass housing.*

5. Urban Neighborhoods: Preservation Begins at Home

The urban neighborhood is architecture in concert: no single structure but an assembly—row upon row of brick townhouses, avenues of staccato three-deckers, rambling Victorians on the tree-lined streets. And the places where the homes meet—"squares," "corners," or "centers" animated by a grocery store, a pharmacy, a drycleaner. As much as the "quaint" green, the picturesque waterfront, the rolling farmland, urban neighborhoods define New England.

However profound this link between the New England neighborhood and New England's identity, by the mid-twentieth century these enclaves had eroded, and with them, New England's sense of self. One had only to scan the front porches to see the attrition of the place countless New Englanders called home. Public face and private space, the porch both symbolized and

Brownstone stoops, rhythmic rails, and flowing bays in an urban neighborhood in Boston's South End.

stimulated the life of the neighborhood. Sagging, rotting, peeling, sometimes even ripped asunder, these porches now spoke with equal clarity of the urban exodus. The all-American rush out of town to split-level living had decimated the urban neighborhood. In the new suburbs, the carport became the public face of the house, and the rear deck, secluded from the neighbors, its private space. America had rejected urban values. Stigmatized by poverty and crowding, disdained for their "ugly" Victorian architecture, old neighborhoods withered.

With a myopia matched only by their self-righteousness, city officials looked to end the blight. Planners imbued with the Corbusian principles of the tower in the park as the ultimate design for living offered the solution: tear the neighborhoods down. The federal government had the

Porches—the locus of neighborliness in this 1940s photo of Southington, Connecticut, above—languished as neighborhoods like Roxbury's Washington Park declined. Urban poverty led to neglect; finally a road-widening destroyed the houses below.

means: urban renewal. Purposefully, they proceeded to eradicate the neat queues of streets, erecting isolated, faceless structures in their stead. The harmonious if ragged houses vanished; large blocky buildings, surrounded by asphalt, appeared. The once-coherent environment was fragmented. The small shops and their owners were scattered. The planners' "solution" had created a panorama that rejected the past and threatened the present.

Slowly, though, new forces gathered. Residents began to revolt. Urban renewal didn't resolve neighborhood problems: it simply removed the neighborhood. And, as the 1960s ran their course, respect for the old and distaste for the new grew. The children of the generation that had bought the postwar dream of a safe and sanitized suburb tenanted by families with 2.3 children and a dog named Spot opted for more open, more urban lifestyles. They began to look beyond the blight of the place their parents had left behind, began to see generous living spaces and interesting decorative details, easy proximity to work downtown, closeness to neighbors. And porches. Once again, their welcoming archways stirred the imagination, signifying neighborliness and community. Drawn by these amenities, the coming generation joined the survivors in the urge to protect and revive the place their forebears had called home.

Predictably in this region that worships early ancestry, it was the most antique, the Colonial or Federal enclave, that appealed first. Beacon Hill in Boston, College Hill in Providence, and others awoke in the 1950s. Genuine treasures from the region's glory days, these were among the first New England historic districts. Protected by legislation stopping demolition and out-of-scale development, discouraging unsympathetic alterations, and encouraging paint and line-by-line restoration, they soon took on a polished look. That look, in turn, drew homeowners. Whole streets blossomed with the cleanup, fixup; the neighborhoods came back.

So did other appurtenances, however. In a pattern that would become a cliché, gourmet markets to feed the newcomers and salons to groom them entered the neighborhood. More problematically, higher rents, property values, and taxes pressured the old neighbors. In the end, the process put a new word in our vocabulary: *gentrification.*

To some residents, "historic district" became synonymous with "elite neighborhood." Historic districts, they feared, would price their homes out of their hands. Was it better to be removed by the gentry than by the redevelopment authority? If urban renewal was death by destruction, was preservation killing with kindness? Or were there tools to revive the life of New England's still neglected neighborhoods without evicting the old neighbors? As historic districts have proliferated and proved their ability to

Graced by the ivy of the ages and the care of recent renovators, the New Haven Historic District off Olive Street flourishes. Proclaiming their vigil against crime and their war against cars, these signs suggest the protectiveness such districts inspire.

Zealous—some say overzealous—restoration brought a clean-sweep look to houses on New London's Starr Street, here seen both before and after.

safeguard their architectural heritage, preservationists and neighborhood activists have sought to resolve these questions.

College Hill Comeback

On a balmy spring day, Benefit Street on Providence's College Hill seems to typify the kind of coddled environment under question. The ample homes tucked into small yards, the soft Williamsburg tones on clapboard, the burnished brass knockers, bespeak generations of loving care. The offhand way the campuses of Brown University and the Rhode Island School of Design intermingle with the historic houses of the Hill reinforces the impression of a privileged history, a happy confluence of the academic and the architectural that is the ultimate New England definition of the good life.

If it is hard to picture the less-than-good life that predated today's scene, it was nonetheless real, for College Hill too felt the erosion of urban neighborhoods in the 1950s. Behind the somewhat Bohemian air lent by students and artists, the neighborhood "was really a terrible slum," Providence preservationist and historian Antoinette Downing recalls. "Five and six people lived in one room with a single toilet in the basement and space heaters to keep them warm." The growth of Brown and the Rhode Island School of Design threatened the area. Concerned more with campus expansion than historic worth, these universities viewed College Hill as raw space filled with dilapidated buildings that should come down. The community agreed. Down with the old was the consensus. Down it came.

By 1955, the defenders of old architecture started to respond. When Brown planned to demolish still more buildings and the city broached urban-renewal plans, pioneer preservationists mobilized. John Nicholas Brown, descendant of the university's founders,

The Woods-Gerry house, designed by Richard Upjohn during the Civil War, almost succumbed to the bulldozers as schools overran Providence's East Side.

Providence's splendid 1907 Armory lends its name and its monumental presence to the Armory District. Using a revolving fund, the Providence Preservation Society plans to conduct an architectural analysis of the deteriorating but splendid structure to begin its preservation.

and the formidable Downing called a meeting to organize resistance. From the first meeting came the hundred-member Providence Preservation Society. From the society's work with city and federal agencies came a classic document: The 1959 *College Hill: A Demonstration Study of Historic Area Renewal.* The first systematic study of how to preserve a historic area, the College Hill report urged a multifaceted approach of public and private investments and controlled university growth. Above all, the preservationists called for "historic-area zoning" for a large portion of College Hill.

The wheels of the bureaucracy ground with unac-

customed speed. Citing goals "sufficient to constitute a public purpose," the legislature agreed. It accepted the tenets that would guide historic districts everywhere: safeguarding the heritage of the city, stabilizing and improving property values, fostering civic beauty, strengthening the local economy, and promoting "the use of historic districts for the education, pleasure and welfare of people." In 1960, it passed enabling legislation. A year later, Providence enacted the College Hill District with a seven-member commission to oversee it.

While these Providence preservationists gave voice to the political solution, others put their money

and their hands to work on the streets of the city. The Burnside Corporation, formed by another sturdy preservationist, Beatrice Chace, bought seventeen houses along the decrepit northern end of Benefit Street, restored their exteriors, and cleaned their interiors. Then, expectantly, the corporation's members set out FOR SALE signs—and waited. Three years went by before the first house sold. "People were afraid of them," Downing remembers. "I was afraid they would all fall apart again before anything happened." Nonetheless, the dramatic spruce-up drew local and national magazines. Before-and-afters filled their pages. "New Life for Yesterday's City," the January 1960 *Architectural Forum* proclaimed. The image of the neighborhood changed. The cycle began: homeowners bought the Burnside houses, allowing the corporation to buy and restore still others, thus encouraging other buyers, who further financed Burnside's work—and on and on.

Still, the forces of demolition didn't retreat. Within a year of the creation of the commission with Downing at its helm, the Rhode Island School of Design challenged the law; the school wanted to tear down the Woods-Gerry mansion. Uncertain of the commission's support, Downing went to the meeting carrying two written responses: one to dissent from the commission if its members voted demolition, the other to support the mandate if they voted for salvation. The savers won. The commission denied the school's request and made its denial stick. Today, the Woods-Gerry mansion, fully restored, houses the school's administrative offices and a gallery. In 1982, the school, an after-the-fact convert, conferred an honorary degree on Downing.

The days when anyone would contemplate tearing down such a superb structure on College Hill have gone. So, unfortunately, have the people who lived there at the time, and Antoinette Downing is the first to concede the tragic displacement. Banks simply

would not give mortgages to poorer owners, she says. Here as elsewhere, preservationists, concerned more with buildings than their inhabitants, had no programs to support existing neighborhoods. Such tools would come later. In fact, the Providence Preservation Society would forge some of them.

Across town, in the Victorian neighborhoods to the west, the society itself has come to the rescue of such old neighbors. Since 1980, its revolving fund has given more than twenty-five grants of about $10,000 each to help owners of the Broadway-Armory district's high-style houses retain rather than relinquish their homes. The society has hired carpenters to teach their skills and has worked closely with a younger agency, SWAP (Stop Wasting Abandoned Property), an organization dedicated to salvaging vacant structures.

SWAP, a grassroots cadre founded to keep both neighborhoods and neighbors intact, began in response to an arson crisis in the 1970s. "When Mayor Cianci was first elected, he made an announcement that he would solve Providence's problem with burning buildings by tearing down three hundred houses," James Boylan, head of SWAP, recalls. "People thought that was not so good." With VISTA volunteers and no budget, SWAP adopted the buildings on the mayor's hit list.

Across the interstate from College Hill's more affluent environs, blight and derelict houses scarred the west end and south side of the city. Vacant and delinquent on taxes, such boarded-up "eyesores" lowered neighborhood morale and often ended their lives as fire-gutted ruins. SWAP took these orphans and tried to find homesteaders for them. In the decade since its founding in 1976, its members have transformed five hundred would-be ruins into restored houses. With state and private sources funding a $150,000-budget, their staff of six helps owners finance and fix forty such structures a year. Whether

the object is a modest three-decker or the grandiose 1885 Gothic mansion of Samuel B. Darling, the revival works for the good of both the individual structure and the entire street. Five hundred abandoned houses still depress the city, by Boylan's estimate, and the number doesn't shrink. Absentee landlords, poverty, and other social ills are beyond the power of preservation, he says. But the houses saved here symbolize today's true neighborhood preservation. From Maine to Massachusetts, from the Greater Portland Landmarks to the Cambridge Historical Commission, today's architectural advocates recognize that the best work of reviving "yesterday's cities" reckons not only with the architecture but with the inhabitants. Their programs help urban neighborhoods not in a clean sweep but structure by structure, enlisting their residents and benefiting them, too.

Boston's South End Saga

Boston's South End is the classic urban-renaissance story writ large. A New England neighborhood on a grand scale, the South End is the ultimate—in terms of size (one square mile), in terms of population mix

Bringing important self-help skills to Cambridge neighborhoods, the vanguard Cambridge Historical Commission's work ranges from low-interest loans to advice on the care and tending of handsome single-family homes or this 1890 four-decker turned office building, shown before and after.

(the most racially diverse in the region's most racially diverse city), in economics (upscale and low-scale), and in quality of urban design and architecture.

The setting for this volatile mix is the essence of Victorian Boston. Street upon street of swell-front red-brick row houses stand punctuated by small parks, their greenery cooled by gentle fountains and encircled by cast-iron fences. Framed more than a hundred years ago by a generation with the skills to shape such niceties, the South End was designed to entice the "better sort" of citizens to stay in town. Faced with an influx of impoverished immigrants and an exodus of affluent taxpayers to the emerging railroad suburbs, the city fathers created a district by landfill just outside the central city. Within its acreage, they planted the English residential park introduced by Charles Bulfinch and popularized in fashionable Louisburg Square on Beacon Hill, then added the up-to-the-minute amenities of public water and sewers to shape the ideal urban neighborhood. Bostonians flocked there, building comfortable homes in the Italianate and French styles then in vogue, and elaborate churches, schools, and institutions to serve their inhabitants.

Success was fleeting: after the Panic of 1873, the area's tone, and popularity, plummeted. In *The Late George Apley,* John P. Marquand's classic novel, the Brahmin father sees a neighbor standing on his front stoop in his shirtsleeves. "Thunderation!" he bellows, and promptly sells his house and moves to the modish Back Bay, then rising on newer landfill across the tracks.

The South End swelled to hold the very immigrants its builders had fled: Irish, Italians, Jews, Greeks, Lebanese, Syrians, Chinese, blacks joined the less fashionable remnants of the original South Enders. In the district vacated by the Apleys, the East European Jew, Mary Antin, spent the girlhood she chronicled in *The Promised Land.* Commodious homes were converted into rooming houses, churches changed denominations, but the affluence that had built the South End did not pass on so easily to its immigrant newcomers. The neighborhood,

now firmly on the wrong side of the tracks, soon had problems. Bostonians documented them in books like *The Lodging House Problem in Boston* and *The Urban Wilderness.* They attempted to deal with them by forming some of the nation's earliest settlement houses. But the neighborhood's status, shaky in the last quarter of the nineteenth century, weakened still more in the twentieth.

By the 1950s, the neighborhood had hit bottom. Gaptoothed streets with rubble-strewn lots, bowfronts disfigured with jerry-built storefronts, and houses abandoned by absentee owners stood vacant and fire-gutted. A hundred and fifty bars lined the seven blocks between Berkeley Street and Massachusetts Avenue. An estimated twelve hundred rooming houses jammed the city's poor into this square mile of space. However elegant the architecture, life for the thirty-six or so ethnic groups sheltered here was devoid of amenities. Many saw the South End as an endangered environment. "We had a burnout a night," Alex Rodriguez, then working for the Emergency Tenants Council, remembers.

In the early 1960s, the Boston Redevelopment Au-

Boston's Chester Square was laid out with a splendid fountain and an urban bosk, as seen in the 1860s. The square was flattened for highway widening in the auto era, while the houses across the street from it fell victim to neglect until recent times.

thority aimed the heavy artillery of urban renewal at this "slum." By then, however, the neighbors knew enough to construct a defense. They had seen urban renewal flatten the vibrant neighborhood of the West End. They saw the replacement of its vintage if somewhat worn houses with the grim highrise paradise of Charles River Park, soon to tempt wealthy suburbanites with a sign that declared: "If you lived here, you'd be home now." Wholesale clearance held no appeal. South Enders were home, and they wanted to stay there.

At about the same time, a new breed, the so-called urban pioneers, arrived. Mostly young, mostly professional, mostly white, drawn by prices of $3,000 to $5,000 for a twelve-room house; intrigued by the Victorian architecture and pleased by the convenient location, they began to buy a stake in the South End. They, too, feared the levelers.

In an era when citizens everywhere were learning that you *could* fight City Hall, fight they did—at public hearings and demonstrations, with petitions and injunctions. Sometimes they fought each other as well as the would-be renewers: Too little low-income housing, said tenants' groups. Too much for one place, homeowners argued. Give us brick sidewalks, said restorers. Hard to walk on, replied the elderly. More trees, said the newcomers. Hiding places for muggers, leaves to rake, said oldtimers. And so the tug-of-war went on. Put two South Enders in a room and you'll get three opinions, said the local wisdom. Amid such debate, the South End careened toward revitalization.

Confused as these battles appeared, the "close-out" of the urban-renewal program seemed downright surreal: in the end, its federal funds exhausted, the city renewal agency simply declared a victory over poverty and left.

In the mid-eighties, two decades after their work began, the survivors survey the field and tally the results. To everyone's benefit, urban-renewal money has underpinned restoration, replacing century-old water and sewer lines, paving streets and sidewalks, installing streetlights and trees, shaping parks with tot lots and basketball courts. Unfortunately, such repairs also forced out oldtimers by raising rents. Today preservationists count defeats in fine buildings downed and sterile monoliths built; but they record victories in street after street of tree-shaded townhouses, in pristine fountains and fences, and finally in the creation of the South End Landmark District.

Five years in the making, the district reflects today's wisdoms. Recognizing that economic and social diversity matters as much to neighborhood character as Victorian buildings, residents and the Boston Landmarks Commission hammered out a district ordinance to protect both. They created a design-review commission from diverse quarters of the community, flexible guidelines to minimize economic hardship, and a revolving loan fund to help the needy. A community that still remembered the firestorm days of urban renewal endorsed this defense against the latest threat: overdevelopment.

Threat it is, for in real-estate terms, the South End's hoped-for upturn has spiraled skyward. Single-floor condominiums now sell for twenty times the price that full houses brought in the 1960s and twice those of the 1970s.

As prices soar, the squeeze for space does too. "Condo conversions" abound, altering both the architecture and the ambience of the neighborhood. Developers plop penthouses atop the graceful roofs, excavate front yards for basement entrances, and pave backyards for cars.

The district can control such architectural debasement. And yet, for all its special tooling, it cannot control social change or economic pressure. Will success spoil the South End? Many fear so. Latter-day condominium owners, they say, don't have the same sense of the street or commitment to the neighborhood. Newcomers lack the pride of ownership or pioneer instinct that sent early homesteaders scurrying to pick up papers and groom parks. Will prosperity flatten the diversity of the old days into a single affluent lifestyle? "It is the natural evolution of life," Susan Park, former head of the South End Historical Society, concedes sadly.

Half-empty for years, the house at the corner of Rutland Square undergoes rehabilitation to match the attractiveness of the square itself. Will such success end ethnic and economic variety?

"In political terms, competing interests in a pluralistic society lead to compromise—even when urban design is the issue," Alex Rodriguez agrees. Yet Rodriguez, who now heads the Massachusetts Commission Against Discrimination, is more sanguine about the change. All neighborhoods evolve, Rodriguez says. He gauges the turnover in the South End at 30 to 40 percent every three years. "My goal for the South End was choices, the more choices the better," he says. And even with today's six-digit speculation, diversity exists. "Gays are accepted. Elderly are accepted. Blacks are accepted. Latinos are accepted. Everyone is accepted." In a city, and a nation, afflicted by racism and other forms of nonacceptance, the South End's capacity to live with diversity remains remarkable.

"Mecca for Minorities" was the name of a recent Fogg Art Museum tour of the South End. The architecture of this square mile of Boston endures, but will the historic diversity? "Lots of pockets of oldtimers still exist," says Arthur Howe, a preservationist from the stop-the-bulldozer days. "They're still here but they're getting fewer in number because their children are moving out," he says. Pulled out by the lingering suburban dream, priced out by gentrification, this next generation flees its native turf. Yes, diversity and tolerance remain, so far, but their future is uncertain. In the end, and sadly, a noticeable turnover of the South End's vivacious mix of people has accompanied its architectural turnaround.

The South End to the South

While Boston's South Enders worry about too much success spoiling their neighborhood, the South Enders of Bridgeport, Connecticut, fear no such spoilage. Their once down-and-out part of a down-and-out city is happy just to have a foothold on the ladder of revitalization.

Like many urban neighborhoods in industrial New England, South End Bridgeport is a collection of single, double, and multifamily Victorian houses. Unlike other middle-class corners of the region, this Connecticut neighborhood reflects the beneficence and ingenuity of an amazing entrepreneur. P.T. Barnum took his showmanship to the streets here in the 1860s, donating Seaside Park, a tract of land designed by Frederick Law Olmsted and Calvert Vaux, to the city. The city, in turn, laid out streets from the downtown to the park—thus transforming the rest of Barnum's farm estate Waldemere into the houselots of Park Avenue's prestigious oceanfront district.

Whether influenced by Barnum's own house, an extravagant tour de force of exotic Moorish motifs, or simply reflecting the ebullient prosperity of the city in its manufacturing heyday, Bridgeport's South End developed a flamboyant architecture beyond its middle-class character. Single and double houses whose designs were pulled from the Palliser brothers' patternbook, *Every Man a Complete Builder,* lined the streets of the brothers' hometown. Deemed hideous in the first half of the twentieth century, when *Victorian* meant dreadful, this colorful array of Stick Style and other Victorian concoctions would eventually play a part in the area's restoration. In 1981, the Bridgeport Architecture Conservancy and the Museum of Art, Science, and Industry, located on the chic upper end of Park Avenue, mounted an exhibition, "A Gift of Taste: Late Victorian Design and the Pallisers." It lent the stamp of art to the "mail-order" designs of the architect-builders. Simultaneously, as Olmsted's popularity grew, Seaside Park's three miles of parkland along the shores of Long Island Sound became a focus of pride at the neighborhood's front door.

If any neighborhood needed a source of pride, it was the Connecticut city's South End. Squeezed on one side by the University of Bridgeport and on the other by industry, neglected by landlords and the city alike, the South End had become derelict. Imitation shingle and brick, sinking porches, paved yards, and chain-link fences were the visual corollaries of

P.T. Barnum's "Greatest Show on Earth," elephants and all, lent a touch of circus color to Bridgeport's South End.

the poverty and neglect in drug raids, robberies, prostitution, and muggings.

The South End's population reflected Bridgeport's ethnic diversity. Known as "Liberia" in the 1830s for its black population, the neighborhood was mixed in the late 1970s: one-third black, one-third Hispanic, one-third white—the last often elderly, many second- or third-generation descendants of eastern and southern Europeans come to Bridgeport's factories before and during World War I. Some rented; some owned their houses. How could preservationists raise neighborhood housing standards without evicting the neighbors?

Neighborhood Housing Services (NHS) provided one answer. Modeled after a 1968 experiment in Pittsburgh and institutionalized by the federal government in the Neighborhood Reinvestment Corporation, Neighborhood Housing Services exists in neighborhoods in 150 cities across the country. It had, in fact, served Bridgeport's upper East Side before director Charles Brilvitch brought the concept to the South End in 1980. Fortunately for the South End, Brilvitch also brought with him a bias for historic buildings and an enthusiasm for the integrity of the environment and its architecture.

With the clout of the Community Reinvestment Act of 1977, which required lending institutions to invest in their own localities, the group got bank funding. They matched it by securing grants from local businesses for low-interest loans. Then they went to work. With $15,000 in city money, staffers secured flowering pear and golden-chain trees to line the sidewalks. They packaged loans and consulted on purchase, financing, and reconstruction of houses. They helped the poorer homeowners in myriad ways, and the South End showed it. Realizing that historic preservation lent a special aura to such economic aid, Brilvitch and his staffers wrote National Register nominations for three districts with between twenty-five and two hundred buildings apiece, and published booklets and calendars celebrating the history of the area. They devised and worked on restoration rather than unsympathetic but equally costly renovation. "Preservation doesn't have to be for the rich," Brilvitch insisted. "I've never met anybody who wasn't fascinated by Victorian architecture once it's been explained to them."

A mustachioed, cigar-smoking young man in plaid shirt and jeans, Brilvitch runs an activist shirtsleeve program that innovates. "Love your house—paint it!" announces a flyer. "We pay people to take off siding and repaint—if they do it in Victorian colors," he says. "If they do it themselves, we pay 100 percent of the cost; if they have it done, 50 percent."

Walk along West End Avenue or Atlantic Street today. "This was deteriorated," says an NHS staffer, pausing at one building. "This was a rooming house," assistant director Deborah Fleisher goes on, pointing to a splendid structure where the color scheme accentuates the rich detail of doors, windows, gables, and porches. Work shows, and is continuous in many of the twenty streets of Bridgeport's South End.

The variety is more than trim-deep. The eclecticism of the architecture matches the ethnic mix. Bridgeport's South End still clings to its diversity. On cism of the architecture matches the ethnic mix. Bridgeport's South End still clings to its diversity. On a sunny spring day, an elderly man sweeps a sidewalk dappled with the shade of an infant tree. Nearby, two young men fix a car parked by the curb. A family sitting on the porch speaks to them in Spanish. Displacement? "We've only displaced the kind of people you like to displace," says Brilvitch, "drug pushers, hookers, the criminal element."

Blacks, Spanish, and whites, old South Enders or new, maintain a balance, and as the neighborhood regains its confidence, it tries to address problems at its borders, too. The University of Bridgeport, a large landowner, and in the past a bulldozer, feels pressure to become a better neighbor. The Friends of Seaside Park tackle cleanup and planting; in the harbor, they have turned a trash-littered island into a wildlife refuge. "The South End has tremendous advantages," Brilvitch notes: the park, the university, the store of nineteenth-century housing. But it is the Neighborhood Housing Services that joined these fragments to the resources of government, local businesses, and residents, shaping a whole to help a whole neighborhood. In so doing, this grassroots group has not only revived its own South End but become a model for all the South Ends of New England.

Seaside Park, designed by Olmsted and Vaux on land given by P.T. Barnum, receives attention from landscape preservationists and boosts the South End neighborhood at its edge.

*As urban renewal claimed urban New England,
moving "just around the corner" meant more than
merely relocating.*

6. Downtowns: Conserving the Core

All roads once led to down-town. "One has the sense that houses were scurrying through the streets of Salem and that those streets were paving themselves," the Reverend William Bentley wrote of his growing town during the eighteenth century. Mercantile hubs in the eighteenth century or manufacturing centers in the nineteenth, the cities and towns of the six states were the pride of the region; at the end of the century, the pace seemed to quicken. Daytimes, the trolleys carried passengers to the teeming center, and evenings, walkers jammed its thoroughfares. "Thousands of shop and factory girls throng the streets glad to catch a bit of fresh air after the confined labors of the day," wrote an observer describing Providence on Saturday nights, when "the entire population seems to be on the streets, some marketing, some shopping, and others walking merely for recreation and pleasure."

All roads led to New England's nineteenth-century downtowns. Here, Boston's Washington Street.

In the twentieth century, they rolled up the sidewalks. As shipping declined and the mills departed, downtown emptied. Poverty plagued urban New England. The imposing banks, elegant insurance offices, and flourishing shops of the early twentieth century closed their doors. With the end of World War II, city life reached its nadir: New Englanders took to their cars, and the cars took them away from downtown. The flight of the postwar generation hastened downtown's demise; urban renewal flattened its remains to extinction. Buildings whose offices and stores had once enticed workers and shoppers fell for parking lots intended to pull them back. To no avail. Why park there anymore? Downtown was down and out.

In the seventies and eighties, the exodus slowed. The growth of high-technology firms and service trades restored the economic underpinnings of some

In Boston, the federal bulldozer flattened the so-called slums of Scollay Square and West End to make way for vast and often sterile new buildings: luxury housing and government offices.

downtowns. Restoration began to replace demolition; returnees began to promote rebuilding. But the back-to-the-city movement was not a panacea. Writ large, it carried its own dangers; the economics of prosperity would put old buildings to a still more severe test. If poverty had endangered historic structures through the attrition of underuse, prosperity menaced them through overdevelopment.

In the center city, where the land beneath buildings has a high value, historic structures face a strange balancing act: too much development, and prize places fall victim to the bulldozers of builders; too little, and they succumb to demolition by neglect. Whether the wrecking ball that ends their days belongs to a developer or a parking-lot proprietor matters little. Either way, downtown still does a dance of death and life. Thus, while many New England cities try to coax business back downtown, others need to ward off developers. For the front-runners in urban revitalization, boom is as risky as bust.

Will Boom Bring Bust?

Boston could be the exemplar of this rags-to-riches-to-ruin story of New England's "successful" cities. In a twist of fate, the very success of the city's preservation efforts for two decades has contributed to the prosperity that augurs ill for the preservation of its historic character.

The story began at mid-century. The moldering downtown of the fifties became the "slum" city

eradicated in the sixties. From Scollay Square to the West End, the federal bulldozer scraped away vivid after-hours enclaves and lively ethnic neighborhoods. Urban renewal wiped out the urban core. A vast government center rose on the site, surrounded by luxury apartments. "Making Way for Progress," a newspaper headlined the demolition. A slash-and-burn attack, said preservationists. As more buildings fell, times changed. Criticism mounted. At length, the urge to preserve became a positive force.

Fortunately, urban renewers had bypassed the larger part of the city, leaving the retail district and much else intact. Bostonians now rallied to save the

Bryant and Gilman's Old City Hall, close to its "last hurrah" in front of the bulldozers, became a preservation victory in 1969, proof that old buildings could be viable.

rest. In a dramatic near-miss, Architectural Heritage, enthusiasts of old buildings, rescued the Old City Hall from demolition in 1969. Reinvigorated, it maintained its majestic stance on School Street. Three years later, preservationists responded to the threat to the *Record-American* building; another "white elephant" became chic. The examples paid off. Quietly, visionary "recyclers" began to tuck retooled offices into languishing buildings, to spruce up seedy quarters. Soon Boston was earning praise as a "second-hand city," a leader in what the phrase of the hour called "adaptive reuse."

In 1976, the project that would become a classic in reuse opened. Faneuil Hall Marketplace made food-on-the-hoof (amid butcher block and brick) a trend. The restoration of the landmark further softened skeptical realtors and bankers. Slowly, developers came to see rehabilitation as an option. By the early 1980s, federal tax incentives made it a more attractive one.

Refurbished architecture of every century housed new tenants. The Ebenezer Hancock house, a pre-Revolutionary building in the equally historic Blackstone block, held law offices in its original Georgian paneled rooms and boasted a compatible addition. The nineteenth-century Ruskinian Gothic Bedford Building, restored to life, had sympathetic storefronts constructed in its once-disfigured ground floor. The owner of the 1929 Art Deco Batterymarch Building even hired art students to revive its gilded decorations; other workers painstakingly cleaned its thirty tones of brick. (Shading from chocolate at the bottom to palest beige at the top, architect Arthur Kellogg's 1928 device gave the illusion of soaring height without breaking city height restrictions.) The cachet of these restored structures and a booming economy made downtown Boston the "right address" once more.

Once home of wholesalers of meat, fish, and produce, the Quincy Market, refurbished by the city and developed by James Rouse, became an urban mall that lent momentum to Boston's revival.

Nonetheless, trouble loomed. While offices with historic images found a market, the demand for high-rise space at the right address also proceeded apace, and the notion of keeping any height limit by legislation was long gone. Gradually, intrusive towers loomed above the old streets. At first slowly, then to the ever-increasing sound of pile drivers, the number mounted. Bringing shadows, wind tunnels, crowds, and an inhuman scale, such mega-structures undermined the very ambience of the city. In the eyes of many, their tone, their texture, their size overwhelmed the historic scale and context that defined downtown as much as any single structure.

To the mayor and the Redevelopment Authority, they meant business, however. For sixteen years, Kevin White encouraged the towers to rise where they would, uncontrolled by zoning or historic context.

Appalled by the existing mammoths and their predicted increase, Boston preservationists gradually began to shout "No more!" By the 1980s, the Boston Preservation Alliance had gathered strength to help them do so. Founded in 1978, the alliance united more than thirty organizations, from neighborhood groups to the Massachusetts Historical Commission. They led the fight. Alliance activists spoke adamantly against highrise construction. "Overbuilt," the Citizens Coalition for Sane Urban Development chorused; "Boston is being looked at as a money machine." "Manhattanization," others called it, a phrase of peculiar power in Boston, conjuring a sibling rivalry of three centuries' standing. For Bostonians, to become a second-rate Manhattan was not to become a better Boston. High on everybody's short list of special American cities, Boston is too intimate, too finely detailed to tolerate the super-scale, they argued. But the city agencies paid little heed: zoning was still ignored, and the intrusive towers sprouted from the drawing boards.

Ironically, such concerns crystallized in a battle among preservationists themselves. The Boston Landmarks Commission, created in 1976, and able to designate single landmarks but not whole districts downtown, found itself dead center between advocates and opponents of highrise growth.

Not surprisingly, the controversy started at the hottest site and rightest of addresses in the city: the "100 percent corner in New England," where historic

The stylized Batterymarch Building. Blessed with changing times and a preservation-minded owner, the structure was restored in the mid-1980s.

BOSTON'S NEXT OFFICE BUILDING, declares the sign on the Federal Reserve Bank before its 1979 demolition in the boom that still threatens Boston.

State and Congress streets meet. It was there that the Exchange Building, a splendid structure and elegant piece of streetscape built in 1893 by Peabody and Stearns, stood, and it was there that development threatened. In the late 1970s, this structure became the focus of the preservation battle. Here would-be saviors looked for landmark designation, but the Landmarks Commission, fearing that a mayoral veto of designation would cause total demolition, offered a compromise: designating only the building's L-shaped façade and forty feet behind it inviolate, the commission allowed the developer, Olympia York, to demolish rear portions and insert a giant glass tower behind the historic façade. "Prosthetic architecture," *Boston Globe* critic Robert Campbell called the design. "Façade-ism," critics complained. "Stage-set architecture." "Better than losing the whole building," commission members retorted. But looking at the glass monolith as it loomed over the low-scale masonry site, both sides agreed that the result was a "visual mishap."

In 1983, the issue surfaced once more with even more virulence. This time it was at Kennedy's Department Store on Summer Street, the city's historic shopping way. Once again, the commission compromised, allowing developers to insert a tower behind the façade of the threatened structure. Though the commission set some ceiling on height and design, its denial of landmark status for the structure gave a go-ahead for a repeat performance: a tower behind a historic front.

Outraged by yet another concession, defenders of both the handsome high-Victorian building and the streetscape came out in force; the most bitter infighting Boston preservationists had known ensued.

The delightful Proctor Building's human scale is dwarfed by its highrise neighbors.

Preservationists had condemned the earlier Exchange Building compromise in vain. Now, stronger in force and feeling, the alliance took the Kennedy case to court. As disheartening as the legal loss and the sight of a scant two floors of the old store suspended in space during construction, however, was the sight of preservationist locked in combat with preservationist, instead of engaging their mutual enemy—mindless development.

To at least one urbanologist, the struggle was not only sad, but a sign of the times. Such jousts, says Rob Hollister, chairman of the Department of Environmental Studies at Tufts University, "are just a testa-ment to our inability to resolve things, a confession of our impotence." And the contorted buildings that result from them are a testament, too, Hollister says, "a visual statement of a very schizoid period and a confused view of change." They will be seen in history as a summation of "the 1970s and 1980s, when we couldn't decide what to do."

What to do, then? "The ultimate solution, of course," says Marcia Myers, executive director of the commission during the fracas, "is preplanning," based on the commission's survey. Planning, the discipline of managing growth and change, means giving consistent direction on where and what and when and how to build. Such planning had not existed since the early sixties, Boston's doldrum days. Since then, planning had disappeared in the urge to lure developers downtown. A historic city, a city rich with architects, planners, and their schools, one packed with trend-setting preservation projects, lacked both a strong planning agency and a comprehensive zoning plan. Thus, the protection of the city's urban environment and quality of life had fallen totally to the preservationists.

To attack this root problem, alliance members sat down with the Landmarks Commission and the Chamber of Commerce to draft amendments to the commission's statute, strengthening its hand downtown. A prime goal was to empower the commission to designate districts downtown and create a rational preservation plan—to stop fighting brushfires and to save the downtown from a highrise holocaust. On the citizen front, alliance activism did not abate; in fact, the group redoubled its labors to persuade an enlarging public about the congestion and eroding quality of life in an overbuilt Boston. Staging hearings, suing to enforce environmental-impact laws, preservationists tried to open new fronts in the battle against the encroaching monoliths.

Newburyport's Inn Street before its revival—vacant buildings, wires, and a down-and-out air.

"Clearly, we've made progress since the sixties," said Stephen Daley, realtor and alliance member, summing up the results of the last decade. "Nobody would dare try to grab off the number-one buildings, or even the second-level ones, anymore. But there's more to the character of the city than a few monuments." Despite an arsenal of state-of-the-art preservation weapons wielded by seasoned troops, despite some hopes that a new Downtown Plan will quiet the building boom, Boston still hangs in the balance. The problems of unchecked growth press as hard as poverty ever has. And the questions remain: Can preservationists and an urban-conscious community shape a city where past and present cohabit? Or will unreined affluence prove a more potent menace than poverty?

Newburyport's Postcard Preservation

While New England's supercities suffer from overheated development, many of its smaller cities and towns continue to wither from the opposite: a moribund economy. Tiny Newburyport, with a population of fifteen thousand, Massachusetts's smallest city, has not grown since the 1850s. City it remains, nonetheless. Forty miles north of Boston, it is and always has been "urban." Blessed with neighborhoods and a real downtown, it has remained a commercial center for the still smaller, now suburban, towns around.

Newburyport began with a flourish. During and just after the Revolution, the city at the mouth of the Merrimack rivaled Salem and Boston in wealth and political influence. A disastrous fire, the War of 1812, and shifting sands in the harbor killed its trade; the decline of the Federalist party ended its political power early in the nineteenth century. It never

fulfilled its promising start. Even when a few mills brought immigrants and money in the second half of the century, permanent prosperity still eluded Newburyport. In the twentieth century, the shoe factories closed, leaving the port city as dispirited as any milltown upstream.

Poverty often preserves. In the twentieth century, Newburyport's proud past endured in the handsome Federal mansions lining High Street, in the somewhat restrained Victorian residences, and in the solid civic and municipal buildings. The city boasted the country's most intact Federal-era commercial district downtown. But poverty's power to preserve has limits. In 1954, the Wolfe Tavern on upper State Street was torn down; the city could not support a good restaurant. By the early 1960s, the downtown, like so many in New England, was worn and empty. Desperate to revive business, the city's leaders took up the tools of the day: traffic and parking studies proliferated; urban-renewal plans filled the shelves. Too many obsolete buildings, said the experts. Too few parking spaces. It was down with the old architecture, and up with a "phony colonial mall in a sea of asphalt," in planner Paul McGinley's words.

The first dust that settled on their wreckage was

the last, however. "Some people with deep roots and some architects who believed that old buildings were an important part of their heritage were aghast," says McGinley. Must Newburyport's history be erased to save its economy? they asked. No, they responded, and backed up their response with counter-studies and injunctions. Demolition stopped. McGinley took office as planning director and looked at the damage. "That street was wiped out before I got here," he says, surveying the old master plan. "And that was gone. And that." More was slated to go. The plan presented to the incoming director eradicated Market Square and eliminated other blocks of Federal structures. But six months later, the plan itself was eradicated. By February 1971, Newburyport became the first city in the country to use the federal laws channeling urban renewal funds into refurbishing historic architecture. Newburyport rebuilt, and in so doing, became a star in the firmament of restoration.

Today the buildings around Market Square still stand, scrubbed and clean. Lower State and Inn streets wear pristine Federal fronts. Simple arched windows punctuate their façades of warm pink brick. With federal, state, and private funds, restoration has pushed outward from the downtown streets and waterfront. Along the grid of narrow lanes that parallel the river "up-along" and "down-along" from State Street, newcomers strip the asphalt shingles off clapboards and repaint, reclaiming the charm of saltboxes and Federal houses. Now, as in its heyday, much of the city could serve as a stage set for a life of John Quincy Adams, who read law there in the late eighteenth century.

The Newburyport that teemed with life as a mid-nineteenth-century marketplace looks rather barren in a 1970s park shaped by architects.

Nowadays, however, "stage set" is a negative description; and it is precisely this stage-set quality that jars in Newburyport, that lends an unsettling quality. Newburyport appeals, but it lacks reality. The context of the old downtown is gone, critics say. Where is the mix of styles, showing life after 1820? Each era's storefronts once gave the sense of a place over time. The restorers secured only the most striking examples, a sample kit rather than a city: one ornate late-Victorian cast-iron storefront here, one Carrara-glass newsstand in all its Deco gloss there. For the rest, they have encased an 1800s period piece, embalmed façades in perfect Federal. Perfect Federal, as perfect anything, can be perfectly dull—a preservation lecture rather than a place.

The landscaping, too, bears a sanitized, stylized look. Take Market Square. Traditionally a broad, flat meeting place, where pedestrians jostled vehicles, the square, contoured by buildings, has metamorphosed; designers have shaped a space encircled by cars. Everywhere, too, brick sidewalks shout "restoration!" The chic of their herringbone pattern is alien to Newburyport's intact nineteenth-century walks.

Restoration has changed the context of use as well. Ice-cream parlors and carrot-cake purveyors abound. No A&P, though, no hardware shop, no grain store. The basics that once served the surrounding countryside have gone the way of the countryside. "Everyday activities progressively decamp, leaving behind a graveyard of artifacts," planner Kevin Lynch once wrote, attacking such architectural emasculation. "Tourist volume swells, making it impossible to save the site 'the way it was.' What is saved is so self-contained in time as to be only peculiar or quaint."

Quaint, yes, but surviving. Newburyport lives, building on its past, pulling in new people—much as it did in the Federal era and again in the mill era. The new owners and tourists do spend money, create homes, rebuild the city's economy. No concrete-block mall with a K-Mart and ample parking would

Newburyport's sampler of times past: the city managed to retain one Art Deco storefront among the Federal period restorations.

have its charms: the town nestles into gentle hills sloping up from a broad curve in the river called the Point Shore. Well-groomed houses line the Point Shore road, their broad lawns, trellised roses, and ancient yews invoking decades of commodious living. Back of the Point Shore, however, lies the real town of Amesbury: solid workaday Victorian and worn. Like Newburyport, Amesbury had tired of its backwater decades, its derelict mills, its vacant storefronts. Like Newburyport, Amesbury wanted to reach the mainstream of American prosperity. Unlike Newburyport, it chose a quiet course.

The traditional Thanksgiving football game between the Amesbury Redmen and the Newburyport Clippers plays out a deep rivalry between the two towns. In football, Amesbury has usually prevailed; in life, Newburyport has had the edge. While Newburyport has built on its image as the historic seaport, the quintessential Yankee city, high in the stratosphere of New England preservation, Amesbury, lacking a glorious clipper-ship past, struggles with making do, with fixing an inglorious downtown.

At the head of Main Street, a tiny triangular green capsules the town's history: a statue of Josiah Bartlett, native son, signer of the Declaration of Independence, stands before the angular red-brick Saint Joseph's Catholic Church and School, center for the immigrant mill workers. Farther down the main street, past the classic white Congregational Church that faces off against the later Romanesque Revival Episcopal one, lies downtown.

Downtown Amesbury could be downtown Anywhere, New England. Its single main thoroughfare, Main Street, ambles downhill through an odd-shaped intersection looping around a former horse trough. Its side streets angle off toward the old mills and houses. Its inhabitants shop at neighborhood stores. And those stores? Anywhere, New England, too—a collage: sturdy Victorian second floors brooding over blank-eyed, bricked-over fronts, garish signs,

have brought them. No banal commercial redevelopment would have rippled out to the city's historic residential streets or reclaimed the adjacent waterfront. Whatever "prettification" besets the restoration, it has spawned a park and marina, cleared away unsightly rails and storage, and saved enough of Newburyport's Federal commercial center to function as it has historically: as the heart of this historic mercantile city.

Will it wear well? When the patina of age settles on this generation's brick and granite, will the jarring elements fade into the context of the city? Will the slick historic fix of the 1970s become one more chapter in the community's ongoing history? Today's best restorers proceed in other ways. They have a lighter touch, a second-generation style. Yet Newburyport remains a landmark in the urban redo that set us back on the road to downtown.

Amesbury Buys Basics

No one will ever call nearby Amesbury "quaint" or overdone. Just upriver from Newburyport, it does

Amesbury's Main Street makeover includes a design for a Millyard off the square. The mill buildings shown here will blend space for light manufacturing, stores, and offices with housing.

paste-ons, the commercial bric-a-brac of endless "up-datings."

By a quirk of fate, this very mediocrity came to the aid of the town. If Amesbury is not "quintessential Yankee," it could be quintessential Main Street. "Amesbury is exactly the kind of downtown the Main Street Program was designed to help," says Tom Moriarty, director of the National Main Street Center. An ambitious pilot project created by the National Trust for Historic Preservation, Main Street aims to bring just such small-town streets back into the mainstream. It picked the place for its very averageness, says Moriarty. A town with no image.

Amesbury was lackluster, but it doesn't lack resources and location. It could go in many directions: high-tech, resort, commercial. However, the Main Streeters also picked Amesbury for its sense of self. The town had made a conscious decision not to pursue Newburyport's upscale allure, but to keep rent levels and property values down, to hold on to their hardware and food stores.

This attitude fit the trust's program. Starting with thirty small towns across the country, Main Street was designed to encourage local citizens to plan downtown improvements that work with rather than against the character of their native buildings. Cooperating with state and local planners, the National Trust tutors merchants in storefront restoration and assists the community with the hassles of parking, lighting, coordinated store hours, and promotions—mundane chores that make downtown work.

Is Amesbury's Main Street Program making a better Amesbury? Joe Fahey, the town's downtown coordinator, walks along Main Street, and points proudly to Ben's Men's Shop, a whimsical Victorian flavor in its signs. He singles out Terry's Flower Shop and Barbara's Bridal Shop across the street. Further down in Market Square, there is Bossey's Restaurant. "A *good* restaurant downtown has made a real difference, too," says Fahey. H & R Block and the Millyard off the square, both under construction, encourage Fahey. "It took two or three years before there was much visible," he says, "but after the first few fixups, there's a keeping-up-with-the-Joneses factor."

Other Joneses seem to like Main Street these days. The trust's Main Street Program has also served as a model for other towns in Massachusetts, which launched its own Main Street program from mill-town Southbridge to collegiate Northampton. Washington has turned off the urban-renewal money machine that once fed renewal in Boston, Newburyport, and countless other cities. States must channel their scant economic aid wisely. Communities now look to find other means, says Moriarty. "Amesbury represents the logical next step in downtown work."

Model-City Makeover

Equipped with the tools forged in Newburyport, Amesbury, and elsewhere, dozens of New England towns have thus begun to rebuild themselves through preservation rather than demolition. In fact, preservationists are now turning their attention to the very victims of urban renewal. Some, like Haverhill and Hartford, have too little life left to restore; others, like South Norwalk or—that ultimate symbol of the bulldozer era—New Haven, may have retained enough of their historic past to serve as a foundation for the future.

Three decades ago, with urban America crashing around him, Mayor Richard C. Lee of New Haven determined to make his city the prototype of America's urban renewal makeovers. He envisioned slum clearance and harbor fixup, housing reform and retail revival; and he pictured parking spaces, "hundreds, even thousands of new spaces every year for many years."

Aided by Edward Logue, that equally bright, equally aggressive city rebuilder (known later for work in Boston), Lee tooled his mid-century dream into what Fred Powledge would call, in a book by the same name, a *Model City.* By 1967, New Haven led the government-grant list; the city could reckon $790 in federal funds spent for each man, woman, and child (compared to $268 for Boston at the time). "A program unmatched in the country," political-science professor Robert A. Dahl wrote in 1961 in *Who Governs?* Even Jane Jacobs called it "the best of the art and science of city planning" in her *Death and Life of Great American Cities.*

In the sixteen years of Lee's administration, a Washington-sent "new look" appeared: The historic buildings of Church Street came down; a two-story Chapel Square shopping mall stood on the site. A network of highways and connectors penetrated the downtown, and parking lots and garages lined the city. The final vision of a one-mile, seven-story parking structure never made it to State Street, but in the mid-sixties a smaller site was cleared and an award-winning garage, contoured as carefully as any piece of urban sculpture by the dean of the Yale School of Architecture, Paul Rudolph, hit the pages of the architecture magazines.

New Haven was the model of how well-funded, well-intentioned, auto-based planning worked, and, on a raw winter day two decades later, the streets of the city attest to how that misguided planning hit the downtown. By the mid-eighties, the very look of the New Haven landscape gives the last lie to the dreams of the Lee generation: if Newburyport and Ames-

Massachusetts has adapted the National Trust's Main Street program for other towns. Here, Southbridge.

New Haven's Chapel Street: the Globe and Gamble-Desmond buildings hewing handsomely to the urban streetscape were taken down for a banal mall in the 1960s.

bury show evolving stages of preservation, New Haven, seduced and abandoned, has become a model of the folly of the "condemn and clear" philosophy that preceded them. Just off the green that is the heart of the city of 125,000, the Chapel Square mall that was the flagship of urban renewal has failed. Still another set of operators is trying to enliven this dreary suburbanized structure. The parking lots still create sullen clefts between historic buildings. Shoddy modernization and signs scar the façades of the architecture of an earlier day. And, scanning the empty storefronts, the seedy signs, the tawdry peepshow billboards and wig shops on historic Chapel and Church streets, the visitor is not surprised to hear a panhandler's voice say, "Can you spare a quarter?"

Aldrich Edwards, director of the New Haven Downtown Council, escorts you in and out of the odd-lot environment that holds New Haven's (and, in its way, downtown New England's) past and present. He points out the buildings old and new, good and bad. He sees the panhandler and, of course, the rips in the old fabric of the street—the derelict storefronts, the gaping parking lots. He also sees and takes pleasure in pointing out the stitches: the made-over Shubert Square theater district or the New Age enterprises gradually breaking out in old storefronts.

A generation and a lifestyle removed from the mayor who made the "model city," Edwards directs the New Haven Downtown Council with a scaled-down, updated dream—a dream of the 1980s. Housed in the Chamber of Commerce quarters in a fifteen-story box left over from urban-renewal days, the council has coaxed some two dozen businesses, plus institutions like Yale, into a partnership with city officials. Filling the void left by the end of federal monies, the Downtown Council provides or promotes funds to stimulate urban development. Since its founding in 1979, it has drafted planners and financiers to turn the remnants of New Haven's past into the vanguard of a revived present.

Whether joining in a fight to stop the creation of a competing North Haven mall or inviting the sophisticated Rouse Company to purchase and refurbish the Chapel Square mall, the council aims to rejuvenate the flagging downtown of one of New England's most economically depressed cores, but to do so in post-renewal ways. To promote private funding, for instance, Edwards solicited investors to form a limited partnership. The partnership coaxed $400,000 from other investors to begin renovating the Ninth Square, the most downtrodden of the nine colonial squares around the New Haven Green. Then, with work underway, the partnership raised a whopping $7.5 million the next year to pursue its plans.

This master strategy, to "create an urban neighborhood downtown," does not have the exalted ring of Mayor Lee's old urban-renewal notions. The Downtown Council's dream is neither grandiose nor utopian; its success is fragmentary. But it is certainly not a vision of federal angels erasing history to make a clean slate.

Small in scale, private in energy, cooperative in design, and couched in terms of "infill"—an inch-by-inch, tucked-in architecture—the council's plans are urban. They show the concern for the rhythm of forms and the texture of complementary materials that create an urban context. Edwards's vision—grimy courtyards transformed into "mews" and

dreary buildings turned into fern-filled apartments —sounds somewhat quixotic as you survey the still-empty silhouettes. Nonetheless, the downscaled design, the participation of small-property owners, and the financial innovations hold promise. If the Downtown Council can use them to reweave the fabric tattered by urban renewal, New Haven could again prove a model city after all—a model for all the region's cities and towns scarred by the heavy-handed tactics of the recent past.

"Main Street is almost all right." Architect Robert Venturi uttered his famous generalization two decades ago, a revolutionary statement at a time when town fathers thought otherwise. Today, towns and cities across New England affirm that view. The New Havens of New England show the stiff price downtowns paid for a federal beneficence that erased rather than reinforced their innate strengths. The Batterymarch Buildings, the Inn Streets, and Terry's Flower Shops, on the other hand, lend credibility to work grounded in the region's historic identity. New England's cores—from village to bustling hub—need retooling, not replacement. So they proceed—south to Connecticut, where the revival of South Norwalk, once known as the "hole in the donut" of Fairfield County, follows the fixup of six cast-iron buildings; north to Concord, New Hampshire, or Winooski, Vermont, where a community developer praises the renaissance that stems from joining past and future. Problems persist. Populations still desert some downtowns; development inundates others. Nonetheless, enlightened New Englanders now see that the heritage of these urban centers animates the region. They understand that with care given to its historic past, Main Street is more than "all right." It is essential.

A 1980s rehabilitation turned this imposing Italianate building in New Haven into space for offices and shops.

PART THREE
Husbanding the Green Spaces

*A view of the common of Woodstock, Vermont, in the
heyday of improvement after the Civil War.*

7. The Cultivated Landscape: Commons, Parks, and Parkways

The land that greeted the first New Englanders was bountiful but untamed. The "wilderness was the unknown, the disordered, the uncontrolled," historian Roderick Nash writes in *Wilderness and the American Mind*. And so, the settlers cleared and ordered the land to ward off the chaos of Satan, carving out common places as they parceled out private lots, tending to their spaces as to their souls. The covenants of early New England linked land and spiritual life; like matter and mind, they were indivisible.

So, in some way, they remain. Embellished over the generations by rural cemeteries, parks, and parkways, the New England landscape wears the legacy of that attitude. Oases in the dense and developed cityscape, this legacy still comprises the nation's most extended network of cultivated greenery. Whether sprawling and

An early-twentieth-century park that bridged the land between Boston's Back Bay and the Charles River now lies under a twentieth-century highway.

linear (the green ribbon of Longmeadow, Massachusetts), compact and finite (the common of Woodstock, Vermont), formal (Boston's Commonwealth Avenue Mall), commanding (Portland's Western Promenade), natural (Hemlock Gorge in Newton, Massachusetts), passive or active, playground or picnic grove, this verdant heritage enriches the region as much as its architectural one.

Here, as elsewhere, however, the twentieth century has taken unkind cuts at the patrimony of the past. Declining urban tax revenues and the rising costs of skilled labor combined with air and soil pollution have wreaked havoc on the landscape. Crime and vandalism took a toll; so did development. In a congested city, parkland looked like wasted land. Parks became dumping grounds—the easiest, cheapest place to thrust ill-designed facilities:

Boston Common a hundred years ago: with cows banned and the perimeter landscaped, the open space served as a pleasure ground for citydwellers, as it still does today.

a school, a hospital, or a highway. Municipalities hardtopped once-green space. "As a nation, we acted as if the land owned by all the citizens was owned by nobody," says Laurie Olins, head of Harvard's department of landscape architecture; such acts by public agencies are "vandalism."

With the return to the city and the growth of the preservation and conservation movements, parks have found new allies. The same civic spirit that prompted the proprietors of New Haven's green to ban geese at the beginning of the nineteenth century and Charles Eliot to lobby for a system of greenery around Boston at its end, propelled twentieth-century friends of parks to pick up litter and raise funds for trees and, finally, to lobby cities to maintain them.

The Common Core

Of all New England's open spaces, the common was and is a constant and symbol of the region. "The visual and metaphorical heart of the community," a twentieth-century study, *On Common Ground*, calls

it. From the seventeenth century, when common land surrounded the meetinghouse, to a more urban nineteenth, when it was bounded by fences, framed by elegant houses, and groomed from pasture into park, the common was a conscious creation, garden more than untamed land, plaza more than natural preserve. "The trees possess a domestic character. They have lost the wild nature of their forest kindred, and have grown humanized by receiving the care of man as well as by contributing to his wants," Nathaniel Hawthorne wrote. Inspired by the craving for spatial beauty, Stockbridge created the first village improvement society in 1853. By the century's end, some two hundred such societies would reflect the impulse for beautification.

On this domesticated swatch of nature, the town acts out its sense of community. Home of craft fairs and protest marches, bandstands and ballgames, social and antisocial activities, surrounded by the postcard white-spired church, ancestral homes, and more stately public institutions, the New England common has survived into its fourth century. On the Boston Common, where John Josselyn watched the local swains stroll with "their marmalet madams" in 1663, Frisbees now sail across the lawn. On the Cambridge Common, where George Washington took command of the Continental Army, advocates argue for a nuclear-free zone.

Other changes of the twentieth century are less felicitous. A rocket on the town common in Warren, New Hampshire, is a jarring substitute for the cannon of history. Widened traffic lanes erode green edges; a Burger King or drive-in bank replaces the gracious lawns that once framed the gentle surroundings. Some injuries to the common are natural —Dutch elm disease, the 1938 hurricane—but some are man-made—widened roads, electrical wires, traffic lights, parking lots. Some harm it only visually.

Others, like salting the roads, destroy its very soil or, like acid rain, stunt its vegetation and eat away its monuments.

"What is common to the greatest number, gets the least amount of care. . . . Men pay most attention to what is their own. They care less for what is common," Garrett Hardin's *The Tragedy of the Commons* states. The common is a symbol of our inability to care for the public weal, he has written. Shared resources are skimped resources. "What happens in this complex pluralistic society when the original people who were proprietors vanish?" asks planner Ronald Lee Fleming. Fleming's Townscape Institute advises towns how to retain or restore their greens. Working with private and public-interest groups, the institute advises on aesthetics and pragmatics. Hap-

Cambridge Common. In 1830, beautifiers fenced both the Common and the Washington elm, where George Washington took command of the Continental Army.

For all the grace of its vintage gazebo, the common in Keene, New Hampshire, is more traffic rotary than haven.

pily, Fleming and others talk to a growing constituency.

On some commons, the stewardship of the original builders is perpetuated by law. The founders of the New Haven Green wrote a permanent covenant of caretakers for their common. Under its weighty moniker, the Committee of the Proprietors of the Common and Undivided Lands of the Town of New Haven still endures. Listed on the National Register, this historic sixteen-acre green serves strollers, crisscrossing its twin spaces, and attracts twenty thousand and more visitors to its staged summer performances. Working with the proprietors, the New Haven Garden Club has cared enough to replace dead elms with a new breed to preserve the heritage of "The Elm City."

Yet even here, ungainly trespassers have encroached on the surroundings which frame and define the common. The perimeters of the green suffer from the assaults of the twentieth century. The graceful balance of commercial and academic, downtown and residential structures that has long defined the edges is difficult to maintain in the face of wanton development. All but the front bay of Henry Austin's splendid old Gothic City Hall came down in the 1970s. Next door to its remains, the banal modern tower of the New Haven Savings Bank (built, in the words of architectural critic Vincent Scully, to "take advantage of the green") further jars the continuity of scale. "How long such a delicate balance can be held in an age of great urban and technological change remains to be seen," Connecticut historian Elizabeth Mill Brown writes.

Fortunately, such assaults have lately caused preservationists to redouble their labors for both commons and their edges. Sometimes, park enthusiasts are an affluent elite or out-of-towners. Counteracting the wear caused by visitors brought by the tourist boom, the common of Woodstock, Vermont, has had

An immaculate fixup financed by Laurance Rockefeller polishes a historic house overlooking the common of Woodstock, Vermont.

careful tending, and many of its surrounding structures have received zealous restoration from Laurance Rockefeller. Ordinary citizens also take hold. Blessed with two commons, a singular sense of pride, but no prince of preservation, the residents of nearby Chelsea, Vermont, have done it alone. They have held workshops to replant and fix the ragged perimeters of their twin greens.

Town commons untouched by trade or tourists have also won support. "There is a calmness and peace of mind present wherever you are in Royalston," two architects said of the rural Massachusetts town in 1972. A year later, they secured a National Trust grant to keep it so, then wrote a report and persuaded the woman who owned the surrounding buildings to place them on the National Register. Such foresight stabilized the common before development could mar its splendid serenity.

So it goes in many corners of New England. Once, the attitude of Keene, New Hampshire, was the rule: it turned its green into a traffic island. Now, the groomed Waterbury Common, jammed at midday, and the bucolic Litchfield Green are Connecticut's testimony that caring for the center cares for the whole. S. Christopher Scott, landscape architect with Massachusetts's Department of Environmental Management, calls the ripple effect "the economics of amenity." To build further on it, Massachusetts has authorized $7 million for twenty-two cities and towns to restore more commons. Connecticut may also launch a statewide commons program. Everywhere, concern mounts. For every green threatened by a McDonald's that aims to plant its golden arches at its side, another finds guardians and guidelines to ward off commercial blight on its border and maintain its historic core.

The gazebo on the classic Chelsea, Vermont, common is to be restored by the town's citizenry.

Off the beaten track, the common of Massachusetts, is preserved through districting and private ownership of surrounding properties.

The Olmsted Legacy

Heir to the shared landscape of the common, the rural cemetery, and the English residential park, New England was also beneficiary of the prodigious skills of America's prime landscape architect, Frederick Law Olmsted. An artful planner, Olmsted endowed the region with vast and picturesque public grounds, parks, and parkways. Believing that only such zones of greenery could save and sanitize an ever more urbanized America, Olmsted brought the country to the city. More than four hundred of his parks and green spaces filled a developing New England; he transformed the wasted corners of the region into undulating landscapes, punctuated by striking outcroppings of rocks and native plantings. The parks created or inspired by Olmsted and his firm between the Civil War and World War I account for much of the historic beauty of New England today.

Unfortunately, they also show the attacks and negligence of the past half-century. As the parks reached the end of their designed life, vegetation ran rampant and infrastructure decayed, while support surfaced slowly. Yet, here, too, a constituency has begun to appear. "Landscape preservation is really coming to the fore," says Charles E. Beveridge, editor of the Olmsted papers. Emerging as both an academic discipline and a focus of public concern, "landscape preservation is beginning to develop the way building preservation did twenty years ago."

The erosion and subsequent restoration of New Haven's splendid 121-acre Edgewood Park, designed by Olmsted's stepson, John C. Olmsted, is typical. Slight compared to some, its scars nonetheless bear testimony to the swipes of our generation. Drive past the glut of drive-in architectural disasters that surround the main gate, enter by the hardtopped tennis courts and graceless skating rink inserted just inside,

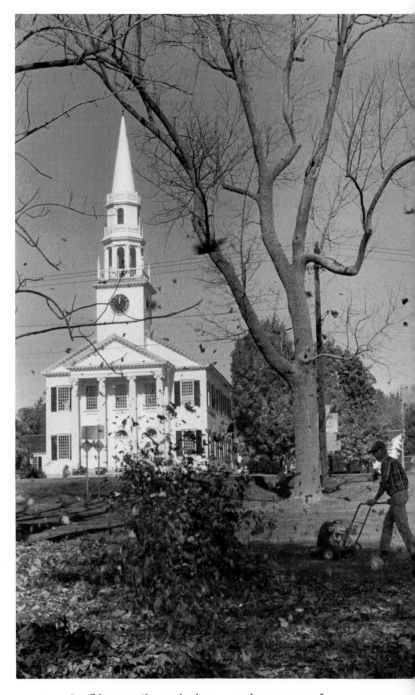

Leafblowers pile up the leaves on the common of Litchfield, Connecticut, where a prosperous community supports such chores.

and you see the blight. "This was originally wetlands and a planned bog garden area, designed to hold storm-water overflow," city landscape architect Robert Gregan says as he scans the site. In 1889, Olmsted's engineering feat had tamed the West River, simultaneously beautifying the suburb at its western gate. In the name of twentieth-century recreation, park planners marred that design to insert playing fields. Supposed landscape "improvements" did still more damage. Awkwardly placed evergreen trees undermined the naturalistic landscape on one slope, and the attempt to excavate and fill a wetlands for yet another playing field left a raw gash in the earth.

And yet, Edgewood endures. Its Norway maples, beeches, and red oaks, its curving paths and rolling contours, have in fact inspired a new constituency. Neighbors have organized and now patrol the park to control cars and motorcycles. They have installed a sympathetic playground and fountain to broaden the park's appeal. Whatever unsightly incursions still scar the perimeters and the entry, Edgewood is a bucolic island, a respite, responding to the care of these advocates.

The story of old intrusions and new enthusiasm for green space that characterizes Edgewood—and other of New Haven's 136 parks, playgrounds, and public open spaces—applies to New England as a whole. Throughout the 1960s and 1970s, the number of caretakers swelled; the ranks of preservationists included friends of greenery along with friends of architecture. The Friends of Seaside Park in Bridgeport, of the Public Garden in Boston, of Lighthouse Point Park Carousel in New Haven, have joined the friends of historic buildings in reclaiming their heritage.

The Olmsted activists span the largest area. Under the far-reaching National Association of Olmsted Parks, they have become the most dedicated work-

Benches are stripped down during the refurbishment of Kennedy (formerly South) Park, Olmsted's design in Fall River, Massachusetts.

John C. Olmsted's Edgewood Park in New Haven. The man-made lake and the trees of this bucolic park have earned a new constituency but still show old scars.

ers for the revival of green space in the region. On the small scale at Kennedy (South) Park in Fall River, Massachusetts, or at the five-hundred-acre masterwork, Franklin Park in Boston, Olmsted parks have gained attention and even resurrection. The Olmsted Historic Landscape Preservation Program, funded by the same Department of Environmental Management that launched the commons' revival, has allocated $15 million to rehabilitate or restore twelve Olmsted parks in eight cities across Massachusetts. Paying homage to the Olmsted firm as repository and source, the National Park Service established Fairsted, his home and office in Brookline, Massachusetts, as a historic site in 1979. It now holds plans and receives visitors and scholars. With 280 designs by his firm in Massachusetts alone, and more than ten times that number nationally, the designer has become, in the words of Olmsted scholars, "an opening wedge" to an awareness of the importance of parks in the cityscape.

Roger Williams's Reawakening

Unfortunately, the very informality and picturesqueness of the parks built by Olmsted and his followers make it simple to overlook them. The gentle contours deceive users into regarding their origins as natural, their fate as inevitable. They question spending thousands to maintain them, or millions to restore them. Many survey the gracious tree-filled acreage of Roger Williams Park in Providence, for instance. They admire the rolling enclave of 430

Enlisting neighbors as advocates and youngsters as a work crew, the Franklin Park Coalition takes on Olmsted's grandest New England park, repairing the neglect of decades in Boston.

create a series of vistas at different turns, the landscape architect shaped the farm into scenery and sculpture, one part water to two parts land. "An enduring gem," in the words of Joel Booden, now landscape architect at the park. "A really wonderful statement of landscape design that has held up over the years." By the turn of the century, Roger Williams Park held forty-seven varieties of birds and animals and an elephant purchased by the pennies of twenty-three hundred school children. Even in 1935, during the Depression, 163 species of trees and shrubs and formal plots of flowers tended by volunteers filled the well-groomed park.

Later it was otherwise. Though parents still walked their children through the zoo or sent them for a spin on the merry-go-round, none cared enough to protest when the highway agency gnawed off twenty acres for an interstate. The neglect dipped to its low point when a bison trotted from the dilapidated zoo and onto I-95. Less spectacularly, the 1896 Classical casino, with its spacious veranda and ballroom, was crumbling. "Structurally, it was a mess," says David Riley, development coordinator in the Park Department's Division of Development and Environmental Services. "The columns were moving off the ground, and the upper floors were falling off the porch."

Though indifferent to the park's malaise, Rhode Islanders couldn't let its casino die. "It was dear to the hearts of the public," says Riley. Thousands of Rhode Islanders had danced beneath its wedding-cake ceiling and savored the cupids in its powder room. They decreed its salvation. Nomination to the National Register in 1976 helped. Public and private funds—$2.1 million—restored the casino. By 1983, the gracious building by Edwin T. Banning again housed gala functions in repainted pastel chambers. Better days had come to this architectural fragment.

Fixing the park followed. "You create an aware-

acres fed by the Pawtuxet River, appreciate the naturalistic beauties the place offers. Few realize, however, that they derive from Horace W. S. Cleveland, an Olmsted follower. It was Cleveland's conscious plan that transformed the raw landscape into a work of art and created New England's largest freshwater park here.

A hundred years ago, Providence was park-poor. With a population of 121,000 and only 121.5 acres of parkland, it had one acre for every 1,000 people compared to Boston's one for every 200 and New Haven's one for every 208. Joining the rush of the late-century park movement, the city hired Cleveland to practice the new art. His canvas was the eighteenth-century farm bequeathed by Betsy Williams in 1871.

Turning swamps into lakes, curving the roads to

Hartford's Bushnell Park: a slum of filth and sewage before a municipal referendum voted its transformation into a park in the mid-nineteenth century.

ness that there is a revolution," Riley says. "Then you turn that interest to the landscape." Restoring other pieces of park architecture made the "better days" still more visible. Preservationists rehabilitated the splendid Dalrymple Boathouse, which now houses the city's park department. They cleaned the bandstand and refurbished the rotunda, a Classical conceit poised in the middle of Crystal Lake with the surreal elegance of an Antonioni movie. Today, Horace Cleveland's landscape also has a following, and less visible but equally vital repairs have begun to undo the erosion of fifty years of indifference.

In the same way that buildings need repointing, repainting, and reroofing, landscapes need care. Where structures require an itemized survey to set priorities, parks need an inventory of their grounds. Landscape historians began to examine Cleveland's plan anew in order to repair the park's condition. With funds from disparate sources—$30,000 in historic-preservation money from the 1983 jobs bill, the same amount in community-development funds, plus services from the park staff—administrators and historians began to evaluate the visual damage, the changes from Cleveland's plan in misplaced roads, and the environmental harm in pollution to his lakes. Their new form of inventory—from plant species to roads and paths, from soil types to computer maps —gave park designers and preservationists a basis for action. Constituency in tow, grounds researched, they can now begin to restore the park and to adapt its landscape heritage to present lifestyles.

Bushnell's Downtown Park

It didn't take a wandering bison or a crumbling ballroom to make Sanford Parisky realize that Hartford's Bushnell Park was decaying. The urban planner then heading the Downtown Development Council saw the crowds who congregated in the park. He also saw its sorry condition: Bushnell Park looked woeful—as downtrodden as the city itself. If any urban area needed a bit of green relief, it was the oddlot environment of the Insurance Capital of America. The barren plazas, pockmarked streets, and faceless office buildings begged for relief. Bushnell Park, sloping from the ornate Victorian state capitol building to the city, gave some respite, but also suffered from blight.

Ironically, it was the same sense of urban wasteland that had prompted Bushnell Park in the first place. One of the country's first public parks, predating New York's Central Park, Bushnell resulted from an 1853 referendum. Its progenitor, Reverend Horace Bushnell, a theologian and mentor of Olmsted, preached "an opening in the heart of the City." Crusading for "a place where the children will play . . . a place for holiday scenes and celebrations," he saw the park as "a place itself of life and motion that will make us completely conscious of being one people."

In the mid-nineteenth century, the detritus of urban life was a more visible affront than it is in our own century. Bushnell deplored the squalor that earned the passing stream the title "Hog River." Sewage poured into the river, shanties bordered it, and railroads, factories, and a tannery added to the environmental misery. The clergyman convinced city leaders to vote for a public bonding. So mandated, Hartford hired Jacob Weidenmann, a Swiss landscape architect, who transformed this desolate site into Bushnell Park. With specimen trees, a romantic pond, and informal paths and plantings, Weidenmann shaped a lovely enclave; and as time passed, the city added to his design. A statue of Winged Victory, a splendid Soldiers and Sailors Memorial Arch, the Corning Fountain, and stone gateways and walls enriched the interior and edges. In the next half-century, the park became "breathing room for the city." So it remains. "What cities need is as valid today as it was when Bushnell prompted this unprecedented public action," says Parisky.

Nonetheless, time—especially recent time—saw Bushnell Park's undoing. In the 1940s, the river was culverted; in the 1970s, interstate highways lopped off six of the park's thirty-seven acres. Walls crumbled. Statues eroded. By 1981, the year when park-lovers founded the Bushnell Park Foundation, their repair list numbered twenty items, from the arch's decaying frieze and walls to water seeping at the reflecting pond. Concrete sidewalks were cracked. Lawns where some 750,000 visitors a year trod needed refurbishing. A grim playground and security fencing lent an industrial air to the landscape. The list went on, and costs went up. To fix just the Memorial Arch would amount to $1 million. Scaffolding alone was priced at $100,000.

In short, the labor to restore the pastoral environment was massive. Aiming to use urban resources, Bushnell's friends solicited contributions to the park from neighbors on its edges. The Parkview Hilton and the Osna Corporation, for instance, which overlook the Corning Fountain, gave money to restore it and renovate the pond. Calling its "campus" the ring of suburban towns around the city, the Friends of Bushnell Park went person-to-person, reaching out to those who remembered, used, or had a stake in the park. Through a *Hartford Courant* "Best of Friends" advertising campaign, supporters raised $300,000 for the pond. By its 5th anniversary, and the city's 350th birthday, the foundation had renovated the Corning Fountain and Hoadley Entrance Way, secured a state-funded brownstone gateway, and installed benches, light poles, and cherry trees.

"The attention that has been paid to buildings is beginning to be applied to public spaces," says Parisky, summing up their campaign. In turn, "the park's been a catalyst for the area that surrounds it and a rallying point for the corporations and the residents there," agrees Michael Kerski, director of the Hartford Architectural Conservancy. "Everyone's for it."

Bucolic Burial Grounds

With such tactics formulated at Bushnell Park, landscape preservationists began to transport their approach elsewhere. Creating a foundation, drafting neighbors, raising funds, and preparing an improvement plan, park activists took the formula to another kind of downtown oasis, Hartford's ancient burying ground of 1640.

A scant two and a half acres, the cemetery on Main Street offers only a demi-haven from its urban milieu. On one brisk winter day, derelicts sleep in the cemetery's corners, and the transactions of two visitors have an illicit air. Nonetheless, here too the public has become more conscious of stewardship. Recruiting neighbors of the burying ground and descendants of those buried there, the venerable Ancient Burying Ground Association enlarged its membership, prepared a restoration and improvement plan, and acted to correct the city's neglect. Despite the inertia of public agencies and private institutions, the focus on this shared space roused advocates. Now, one neighbor, United Technologies, may help finance the repair of worn gravestones and paths.

In this dense New England urban corridor, such cemeteries are secret gardens, a vital and neglected resource. A shared open space, the cemetery, like the common, makes the communal will visible. "In the common imagination, graveyards were one step removed from Heaven, and half a step from Hell," historian John Stilgoe writes, and the aura endures. While their open space provides relief from the unrelenting masonry city, they offer symbolic relief from the urban landscape's axiom of greed—the money-first motives of the realtor's "highest and best use" of the earth.

Cherished or ignored, offering memories of city founders (in Hartford, Thomas Hooker), revealing traces of early art and life, and displaying their sacred origins, these "gardens of the dead" offer a vast potential—but an equally vast chore for preservationists. Boston alone has seventeen early cem-

Boston's Old Granary Burial Ground, where Mother Goose, John Hancock, Paul Revere, and Samuel Adams lie buried, needs care.

eteries. Whether in the heart of the business district, like King's Chapel and the Old Granary, or in today's outlying neighborhoods, like Roxbury's Eustis Street Burying Ground and Charlestown's Phipps Street, they, too, have begun to attract attention.

Final resting place of Puritan divines, Revolutionary patriots and the British soldiers they fought, governors, painters, poets, and even Mother Goose, such seventeenth- and eighteenth-century burial grounds delight anew. With their compelling stone images and pithy sentiments, they also mark the finest artistic expression of the "Puritan centuries." Yet they cannot survive all by themselves. "We can't say, 'They've been around for two or three centuries; they'll last a little longer,' " says Jonathan Fairbanks, curator of American Decorative Art at Boston's Museum of Fine Arts, "because they won't." Every winter, twenty stones go to their last resting place. "You have a little crack in one in the fall, moisture gets in and freezes, and in the spring, it's in pieces," he says. Air pollution and acid rain accelerate time's erasures. The city's beleaguered Parks Department can scarcely cope with the staggering problems of crime and vandalism, crumbling walls and eroding paths. Their scant crew of three maintains all seventeen plots. But here, too, times change. In the mid-eighties, the Landmarks Commission and the Parks Department set to work on the problem: they established a task force advised by a dozen private and public agencies, began a stone-by-stone survey of each cemetery, and appointed a project coordinator. The tasks drew on disciplines from science (how do you save funerary art from decay?) to sociology (how do you enlist the neighbors to become "friends"?). A group of consultants pulled together a master plan. Its listings of engineering, landscaping, lighting, fencing, and stone conservation tasks tally the cost of

safeguarding New England's fragile islands of repose and chart a course for cemeteries everywhere.

Parkway Preservation

If graveyards, the most permanent sign of New England settlement, decay so drastically, what hope can there be for roads, the ultimate symbol of mobility? Yet even some of these roads and scenic parkways have preservation advocates. From the activists who strive to stop a highway from plunging through the historic route of Lexington's and Concord's "Battle Road" (now a national park), to the supporters of the Merritt Parkway, such green highways win backers.

"Parkway Theater" was what historian Pamela Allara labeled the Merritt Parkway a decade ago. "Conceived and executed in the heyday of public art —the 1930s," as she noted, the Merritt was designed by George Dunkelberger, architect for the Bridge Design Unit of the Connecticut Department of Transportation. Like the Bronx River Parkway, it had "the general aim of protecting the natural envi-

Rural cemeteries of the mid-nineteenth century, like Cambridge's Mt. Auburn, provided a model for the parkmaking of a later period and a retreat for city-dwellers, then and now.

*Mossy gravestones in Marblehead, Massachusetts,
tilt under the weight of years.*

The imaginatively designed bridges of the Merritt Parkway's overpasses add to the pleasure of the curving highway.

ronment and insuring a pleasant trip for the traveller," Allara wrote. But even as she wrote, the attack came.

Four decades earlier, in the early auto age, the Fairfield Planning Commission had recessed the road to save those who abutted it from noise and keep auto traffic from spoiling their rich environment. Aiming to maintain "the rural character and residential attractiveness of the country," they built protection, and even beauty, into the parkway's thirty-seven-mile stretch through Fairfield County. Then they punctuated the relaxed ride with vernacular architecture at its most entertaining and eclectic; their bridges enlivened the parkway with reliefs from rustic and Art Deco to classical. Geometric (ziggurat) or naturalistic (butterflies, spiders), they provided a variety of visual experiences foreign to the graceless bridges of later interstates. A trip on the newer, parallel Connecticut Thruway can best be called a survival exercise; a drive on the Merritt can still be a pleasure drive.

Notwithstanding the romance of this road, a mid-seventies widening leveled four Merritt bridges, altering the sense of place. Still other of its sixty or so fanciful bridges were under attack after the state refused to put them on the National Register. Even more blunt and brutal intersections were on the drawing boards. When the walls of famous buildings were tumbling, the call to "Save the Merritt" may have sounded strange, but here too "friends" rallied. Fighting to save the Merritt, preservationists launched a crusade to stop the bulldozers. Activists worked through state and local communities to curtail the wideners.

Today—the fight somewhat abated—admirers still worry about the bridges' slow decay. Insensitive repairs and overgrown greenery may alter and obscure their artistry as much as the bulldozer. Meanwhile, the road's contours still face extinction by straightening. If most of the bridges are "intact,"

according to the Connecticut Historical Commission's environmental-review coordinator, David Poirier, the need to ward off replacements and harmful repairs continues to demand watchdogs.

Will New Englanders summon that stewardship here? Will they do so elsewhere for New England's parks and greenswards? Will commons, parks, and parkways generate the constituency needed to fight the encroachments of man and time alike?

Eternal vigilance is always the price of preservation; but with green spaces, the struggle is doubly taxing. Nature is in flux; the parks and parkways, commons and burying grounds of the region require more constant care than the architecture. Stewards have come to see that they must be especially tenacious in guarding and restoring their cultivated open spaces, that their zeal—only now awakening—must be as long-lived as nature itself.

The Stoeckel estate in Norfolk, Connecticut, serves as quarters for Yale's School of Music and its summer concerts.

8: The Landscape of Leisure: Estates and Resorts

Whether as country seats for eighteenth-century merchant princes or "seaside cottages" for the nineteenth-century industrial plutocracy, New England's fine estates created a landscape of leisure on the countryside. The Victorian era escalated their number and size, with great estates burgeoning in Bar Harbor, Newport, and Lenox. Resort hotels for the many mimicked them in Nahant, North Conway, and Kennebunkport. Centuries before the second homes of our day, this showplace architecture with its gracious landscapes and elaborate outbuildings ornamented New England.

By the twentieth century, though, changing lifestyles, the "servant problem," income taxes, and the cost of heat and maintenance had brought these pleasure palaces close to extinction. In earlier times, New Englanders had secured hard-pressed estates by

The Longyear Foundation of Brookline, Massachusetts, cares for the eloquent Classical grounds and mansion that hold the memorabilia of Mary Baker Eddy, founder of the Christian Science religion.

means of that eternal industry: education. When an estate fell on hard times, someone started a school, or expanded one into grander quarters. In the eighteenth century, an impoverished widow might open a finishing school for young ladies in the echoing chambers of her mansion. In the nineteenth century, proliferating academies and colleges kept the estates going; in the twentieth, religious orders joined them. Even after World War II, the Sputnik era boomed with junior colleges and technical schools. While larger universities built bold modern campuses with language labs and computer terminals, smaller schools still filled out the old estates. In the 1970s, it changed; the loss of funds and students emptied many estates. Ever-rising expenses and ever-changing lifestyles took their toll. So did decay.

Sometimes, it was the structure itself that fell.

Sometimes, the setting deteriorated faster than the building. As developers dissected graceful landscapes into rigid subdivisions, the great estates became shadows of themselves. Their shells and surroundings languished. Their would-be saviors looked for a solution.

Here and there, under the wing of county, city, or regional groups—the Society for the Preservation of New England Antiquities (SPNEA) or one-house associations—some of the handsomest estates survived as museums. Still it was a struggle. Heating oil and new roofs cost no less for good causes than for vain display. "You look at the budget and say, 'Which roof is going to be replaced? What water heater is about to go?' " says Lynne Spencer, director of property management at the SPNEA. To ensure the care and feeding of its house museums, even this august institution has had to rethink its ways. Using preservation easements—clauses in the deed that restrict future change—SPNEA has sold off minor properties to fund larger ones. Estates like the splendid Lyman and Codman houses in Massachusetts, or the Bowen house in Connecticut, strain even their resources and imagination. Only the most fortunate of New England's palaces support themselves by visitors alone. Add lavish grounds, and the equation is more unbalanced. Clearly, making a museum—embalming the white elephant—is not the answer. Such extravagant relics tax any budget. Yet how can we maintain these gems of architecture and landscape design?

Challenge at Castle Hill

A line of cars, sporadic but dogged, turns off Route 1A by the Ipswich Common and follows Argilla Road

The grounds of the Codman house needed costly and extensive restoration for visitors.

*American Gothic enshrined: the Bowen house, also
called Roseland Cottage, in Woodstock, Connecticut.
Its pink house and gracious grounds, built in 1846 as
a summer retreat, still greet visitors, courtesy of the
Society for the Preservation of New England Antiquities.*

through the countryside, past the tree-shaded houses and gardens. Then, where the trees thin out to salt marshes dotted with wooded islands on either side of the road, the cars turn. Through the great iron gates and stone gatehouse, past the guard, they slowly climb the winding drive between rolling fields and stands of oak and beech whose bare branches permit glimpses of the marsh and ocean stretched below. Halfway up the hill the trees part. There, a broad, statue-lined allée rolls downward to the sea on one side and, on the other, sweeps upward past an elegant, if crumbling, Italianate pavilion to a stately mansion on the crest of the hill. In the clearing ahead, deer, grazing in the fading afternoon light, lift their heads to gaze at the cars, then resume their repast, nibbling the short grass through its light dusting of snow.

Finally, at the pedimented door by the gravel courtyard, a trim-bearded man in evening wear stands on the stone step to welcome these guests. Arrayed in the tweeds, velvets, furs, paisleys, turtlenecks, and boots that herald Christmas on Boston's North Shore, they congregate by the fire crackling in the stone fireplace, then file through the tall paneled doors. At last they cross the circular domed anteroom of ornate boiserie into the music room, dazzled by the light from the wall sconces and the fire reflected in its beveled mirrors. The scene is as Baroque as the silver-haired violinist's instrument and the Handel sonata for violin and harpsichord continuo—and as resonant with history.

Seventy years ago, too, cars made the drive; their riders scanned the deer, admired the vistas. "Seventy years ago, Castle Hill was built to offer friends an exceptionally beautiful experience," says the brochure prepared by the estate. "It still does." Today, however, the "friends" are not intimate acquaintances but friends of preservation, friends trying to make Castle Hill a cultural resource for the North Shore, and to fill its treasury as well.

Built by Chicago plumbing magnate Richard T. Crane, Jr., between 1910 and 1928, the vast mansion and its 165 elaborately landscaped acres crown Castle Hill, which covers 2,000 acres of hill, meadow, marsh, and beach in Ipswich and Essex. At its height in the 1920s, the estate employed a hundred groundskeepers to clip hedges, rake the bocci court, tend the lawn, and trim the rose gardens. The next decades eroded the owners' capacity to keep such a staff as fast as it eroded the grounds. By the time the last Crane wrote her will, the life she had maintained on the estate bore scant resemblance to the world of her heirs. In 1949, she bequeathed the vast estate to another kind of caretaker—the Trustees of Reservations.

Founded in 1891 by the visionary young landscape architect Charles Eliot, the venerable Trustees of Reservations was charged with the mission of preserving the most beautiful spaces of Massachusetts as a "museum of the landscape." Its scenic treasures now include seventeen thousand acres of land owned outright, ranging from wildlife refuges to formal gardens, and another five thousand protected through

Money must go toward bringing the main building up to town code requirements and restoring the crumbling brick and concrete work on the once-elegant terrace of the Crane estate.

conservation easements, along with six museum houses. In these good hands, Castle Hill was ostensibly saved for posterity.

But was it? How does a private nonprofit organization dedicated to preserving natural areas maintain an establishment like Castle Hill? The practice of preserving great estates has all but passed. "Land values have gone up so high," says William Clendaniel, deputy director of the trustees. "How many people can afford to leave a million-dollar property and then two million to endow it?" So what was this hard-pressed conservation group to do with a fifty-nine-room mansion devoid of furniture, a swimming pool that leaked, and gardens enough to tax an army of weeders?

In 1951, the trustees created a separate nonprofit corporation, the Castle Hill Foundation, to deal with the house and its 165 acres of outbuildings and landscaped grounds. While the Trustees of Reservations continued to manage the estate's natural areas, like Crane's Beach, the foundation fought to restore and refurnish the house—to bring life and income through concerts and other programs.

The cure almost killed the patient. In the late fifties, the summer concert series grew in popularity, but the ten thousand people who came to hear the Kingston Trio on the Grande Allée in 1961 did so much damage to the grounds and statues that large-scale concerts were stopped. An Early Music Festival and seminars in the 1970s won acclaim but lost money. Meanwhile, the concrete still crumbled and the roofs still leaked.

In the 1980s, the trustees took stock of the decaying estate. "What the design needed was three or four million dollars," says Clendaniel. "A minimum of half a million in immediate needs." The trustees instituted a management program focused on costs, the same bottom-line practices that built the Crane fortune. Then they installed a new director. The re-

sults? "We broke even on our programs for the first time in 1983," says that director, William Conner (he of the trim beard and evening suit). The property-improvements budget has gone up by 400 percent in the past two years, he says. "We've done a lot of work on the casino and stabilized some of the retaining walls. The bachelors'-quarters roof doesn't leak anymore, although we still have a tribe of racoons living in there."

Urbane, versed in music, comfortable with fund-raising and corporate-giving (or nongiving) patterns, the director belongs to today's managerial breed, grounded in the need for great estates to offer "good, solid programs" to survive. Building on earlier musical successes, the Castle Hill Festival's concerts, tours, and following expanded. Winter chamber concerts extended the season. Functions multiplied. The Crane Estate took advantage of the "rent-a-mansion" trend; weddings, balls, bar mitzvahs, and corporate receptions accounted for 50 percent of the foundation's income. Still, the growing constituency itself took a toll. In 1984, inspectors cited the estate for building-code and public-safety violations. "We couldn't flush the toilets one weekend. We couldn't turn on the lights," says Conner. "We spent tens of thousands of dollars." Meanwhile time and crumbling concrete race on.

"There's nothing we can't solve with a million—

Devices from "adopt-a-window" to "rent-a-mansion" produce income at SPNEA's Lyman house and other aristocratic works of architecture. Are they enough?

or two or three," Conner laughs. "There's no endowment. There's no single source of income. The only way to keep this place alive is to use it and use it heavily—within preservation parameters." He cites attempts to broaden the base with school programs and seminars, ecology courses and business conferences. "I like to keep in mind the pattern of an Italian humanist's estate," the self-described optimist goes on. "Grounds of excellence filled with scholarly documents and stimulating people." If, to paraphrase Talleyrand, no one who was not alive before the Depression will ever know how sweet life can be, Castle Hill, like other former haunts of the rich, can give a large number brief tastes of such sweetness. In re-

Repairs totaling $750,000 for Rosecliff's terra cotta are not the least or the last of the expenses for the Preservation Society of Newport County.

turn, those who taste that life will support it—or so the theory goes. The question is: Will it work?

Keeping Up with the Vanderbilts

Castle Hill is not alone in its struggle. Within fifty miles, Hammond Castle in Gloucester holds Christmas concerts; the Gore estate in Waltham uses its grounds and environs for soirées. So does the Lyman house, which also holds plant sales in its greenhouse. ADOPT-A-WINDOWPANE and UPHOLSTER-A-CHAIR fund-raising tags dangle throughout SPNEA's Codman house in Lincoln, signs of the inventive devices needed to lure supporters.

Even without events to coax them, eager architectural voyeurs journey to such millionaire meccas across New England. Nine hundred thousand people a year visit the most opulent of these, the "cottages" of Newport's Belle Époque, run by the Preservation Society of Newport County. Manager of eight of the lingering palaces of the people who turned late-nineteenth-century Newport into playtime at its most architecturally pompous, the forty-five-year-old society is savvy in the way of tours and staged celebrations. And still, its $4.5 million budget barely allows the organization to break even. The upkeep of these ornate establishments—the floors to polish, walls to paint, lawns to groom, and tours to take visitors in and out—requires 350 employees.

"There's always something," staffer Monique Panaggio says. The terra cotta falling off the outside of Rosecliff was a $750,000 "something." So was the recent $700,000 restoration of a 1914 Chinese teahouse at Marble House. A "kind of exclamation point to the Gilded Age," the society called it. That doesn't count the care of interiors in need of constant redoing; again, an endless list. The silk tassels to adorn curtains at the Elms come by a very slow boat from Italy; the patterns copied by the Schumacher fabric house are time-consuming and costly. The detail that delights today came from the end-of-the-century socialites' "drive to outbuild, outstaff, outdress, and outparty their peers," as the preservation society

puts it. It fascinates the observer both sociologically and architecturally, but it stretches twentieth-century budgets.

Consider simply the gardens of such grand estates. A fragile but lovely legacy, they define the environment as much as the architecture. Such splendors as Thuja Gardens in Bar Harbor with its processional lawn are not only an ornament, but, as Elizabeth B. Kassler writes, "an essay in the tenancy of the earth." The true meaning of an estate, then, depends on a sense of spatial integrity that stems from its historic grounds. But in an era when land values soar, development presses, and hand labor is hard to come by, how can preservationists keep up the well-tended greenery of the past?

Estates for Everyman

In populous suburbs or resorts, the trend to parcel estates into condominiums has offered one answer. John Cherol, executive director of the Preservation Society, estimates a quarter of Newport's remaining palaces, sixty or seventy of the three hundred mansions still intact, have been cut up into condominiums or time-sharing apartments since the Tall Ships sailed in to publicize the town in 1976. Newport lacks good zoning, though, so while such divisions have sometimes saved the structures, they have often played havoc with the grounds, transforming mature landscapes into standard subdivisions.

Bonnie Crest, a splendid Tudor concoction designed in 1915 by John Russell Pope, creator of the Jefferson Memorial, underwent just such an assault. Divided with some care because of its place on the National Register of Historic Places, the mansion itself remained a handsome monument. But the developers treated the grounds like a wasteland, adding buildings that sit like barracks on the edge of the lawns. The entourage so destroyed the ambience of the estate that Bonnie Crest was removed from the National Register.

Such attacks on the landscape can mar the environs more than demolition, and as they have multi-

The archway of silver lindens at Newport's Hammersmith Farm—formerly the Auchincloss home and now a tourist attraction—is just one of the many handsome Olmsted landscapes in need of tending and appreciation on such estates.

Harbor, written by Gladys O'Neil, with Bar Harbor Historical Society photos.

The remaining cottages show a range of reuses. Some survive as well-adapted inns or boardinghouses; others display ungainly additions or idle behind FOR SALE signs. The fate of the Bay View Inn, for instance, is mixed. While the developers refurbished the house and gardens with finesse, the same management replaced the mansion next door with a graceless new building. Set in asphalt, the developers' structure looks like "Colonial-Land," produced by Central Casting.

To stop such debasement, preservationists have begun to act on a larger scale. Operating in the photo-filled basement of the Jessup Library, the survey run by O'Neil for the Bar Harbor Historical Society has paved the way for securing three districts —complete streets of houses, great and small. Meanwhile, they work with the town to revise the zoning ordinance to protect Bar Harbor from the heedless commerce that could destroy its historic ambience and present attractiveness. To outsiders, progress seems slow and opposition continuous, but, says Georgia Mavrinac of the Maine Association of Conservation Commissions, "business people are beginning to see the importance of retaining older architectural features. They realize that people are coming to visit Bar Harbor, not the New Jersey shore."

How to protect the integrity of the land? That is the problem that faces Bar Harbor, Newport, and towns with lesser collections of extravagant homes in lavish settings, says Wayne Linker, former head of the Connecticut Trust for Historic Preservation. "The feasibility of incorporating a museum or monastery in such places has passed," he notes. Small successes do occur; Linker cites, for example, the preservation of the Farwell mansion in Norwalk, now the headquarters for a corporation. Yet he worries about the horror stories. The tale of the Darien

plied, preservationists have sounded an alarm. Newport, they insist, is not merely an individual palace or two by a prince of architecture. It is a kingdom, a congregation of castles in a landscape and neighborhood. Finally, in recent years, advocates pushed through a historic district. They further fortified the district by tucking it under the planning department and insisting on review of new designs. "The really bad ones don't get by," says planning commission member Brian Pelletier, describing the results. Still, it's a slow process. "You talk to developers about stone and color. They don't know what you're talking about. They have no sense of what goes with the surroundings." The fight goes on.

Faced with a more rustic catalogue of castles in a less populous place, Bar Harbor, Maine, altered or flattened many of its grandiose hulks over the years. In some ways, New England's northernmost resort epitomizes the passing of the palmy days at the great watering places. Many "cottages" not demolished for tax reasons fell in the "forest fire holocaust" of 1947. Today, only fifty of the lavish dwellings of the last century remain; the rest fill the pages of *Lost Bar*

The summer ambience of Maine's Poland Spring House, a splendid nineteenth-century resort, died in flames along with the hotel.

owner who sliced out thirty feet from the middle of a hundred-foot mansion to make two structures underscores the need for a broader solution. Single private decisions, whether by individuals, corporations, or nonprofit owners, can create environmental havoc and have a dreadful impact on the community. "The need is for informed public planning," Linker says.

"Historic overlays" is one solution, he goes on. Based on cluster zoning, this concept lets towns preserve precious landscapes. By considering such historic surroundings as special cases within the overall landscape of a community, they can tailor zoning to save them. Instead of splitting the rolling lands and plantings into houselots, developers get a variance to cluster their condominiums in one corner. In return, they create perpetual easements on the land. In the end, a segment vanishes, but the look of the landscape endures.

Resort Hotels

If the grandiose houses and gardens of the rich challenge preservationists, the vacation haunts of the less wealthy offer no less a test.

The age of recreational travel dawned in the nineteenth century in concert with the age of railroad and steamboat. With artists and writers in the vanguard, ordinary New Englanders headed out along the lines in search of rural respite. By the end of the Victorian era, pleasure palaces built to attract them sprawled over the mountains and valleys, the lakesides and coastlines of New England.

These public "summer places" operated for only a short season. They were built almost entirely of

A doughty survivor: the 1764 Walloomsac Inn in Bennington, Vermont. Though far removed from the splendor of days when it hosted Teddy Roosevelt, the inn has life and charm beneath the peeling paint.

wood, using the thinnest of walls and the cheapest of the new balloon-frame construction, but their gingerbread ornament, broad porches, grandly scaled public spaces, and glorious views provided glamour. Expanding after each successful season, they soon became rambling labyrinths: hallways meandered around corners; additions sidled up and down hills. Though their charm was undisputed, their efficiency was not; with the passage of years, rambling often became ramshackle, and, as America's vacation habits changed, the charms of these summer places paled.

Some, like Wentworth-by-the-Sea in Newcastle, New Hampshire, or the Equinox Hotel in Manchester Village, Vermont, managed to survive into the 1960s and 1970s by upgrading and building additions. Others, like the Walloomsac Inn, active in Bennington, Vermont, for two centuries, weathered, clinging to life with minimal maintenance. Still others gradually slid into oblivion. True to the "tinderbox" analogy often applied, many succumbed to flames. *The Grand Hotels: Glory and Conflagration,* the New Hampshire Historical Society titled a pamphlet describing their days of splendor and "dramatic downturn." For most, it was less dramatic. They simply

The gracefully sited former Holderness Inn in Holderness, New Hampshire, and the sign that points the way to the Science Center that has no use for it.

The Smith Piper General Store in Center Sandwich, New Hampshire, is part of the characteristic small-town New England ensemble.

sank in picturesque decay, their fate so obviously poised between destruction and salvation that they lent an air of romance to the towns they dominated.

The Holderness Inn near Lake Winnipesaukee, New Hampshire, has that gaunt air. On a summer day, the gray ghost with its wrap-around veranda, its pointed and scalloped shingles, bespeaks an era of languor and grace. *Heritage of Herons* and *Flight of the Whooping Cranes,* two movies playing at the Science Center, its owner lodged in new quarters above the former inn, typify the attractions of nature that draw visitors here today. Notwithstanding, the inn teeters on the edge of extinction. Though "basically sound," in the words of Peter Hendel, assistant director, the structure was threatened by the Science Center itself. Agents of the natural rather than the built environment, they would like to rid themselves of a nuisance that is "expensive to maintain." Even though the inn gives a sense of place to the center of town, it is "irrelevant" to their purposes and "en route to becoming an incredible eyesore," Hendel insisted, rationalizing its demolition. Clearly, a clean-sweep front lawn for the Science Center held more allure than the vintage inn and landscape. By the mid-eighties, demolition seemed imminent.

Moments before that last act, however, an architect arrived with a heroic solution: move the 7,000-square-foot structure. For one dollar, Ward D'Elia of Asquam Lakes Corporation bought the 1880s inn and a year's stay of execution. If the market bears the price, he plans to move the structure to another spot he is developing, called Curry Place. "There's a lot of square footage," D'Elia observes. "It's a good building and we may be able to capitalize on the tax credit," he goes on. "It has character."

Nonetheless, while the old inn may stay intact, the town will lose that character. Whether executed by bulldozers or evacuated by movers, the Holderness Inn will go, and with it an important relic of bygone days. "The site where it is now is the best site," even its would-be savior admits ruefully. Neighbors, though aware of its appeal, can do little to prevent its departure. In fact, only the rare town, like nearby

Sandwich, New Hampshire, can insist on the rules to regulate buildings that preserve the past. The Holderness Inn's story simply offers a wry version of the norm. It is a much-told tale and brings up a much-asked question: Will vacation New England lose the graceful sites and structures that make the journey worthwhile?

Destination: History

Elsewhere in New England, some hardheaded developers have sensed profit as well as romanticism in saving such sentimental relics. The developer of the refurbished Stonehurst Hotel in North Conway, New Hampshire, voices the trend in the language of a new vacation vernacular: "We're going to see a resurgence of the destination resort hotel," Ernest Mallett believes. "Americans are returning to a more relaxed lifestyle, and that includes their vacations." To this entrepreneur, at least, "relaxed" means "historic architecture."

The tiny village of Jackson, New Hampshire (population 500–600), in the Mount Washington Valley, is a good example of New England resort history. In the early years of this century, thousands took the train

Norumbega, a ponderous private estate overlooking Penobscot Bay in Camden, Maine, had fallen into disrepair by the early 1980s. Since then, a new owner's passion for the past and the growing popularity of bed-and-breakfast inns have helped it survive as an elegant vacation lodging.

to the town cooled by the White Mountains, "including national officials, New York financiers and men great in the ecclesiastical and education world," a turn-of-the-century scribe wrote in *With Pen and Camera through the White Mountains. Yesterdays,* a reminiscence published in 1978 by the Jackson Historical Society, counted two dozen inns, hotels, and lodges, as well as house after house filled with summer boarders. Come World War II, the old places shut their doors, eclipsed by the motels along Route 16 between Conway and North Conway. Porches rotted, pipes burst, roofs leaked. The historic portion of the Iron Mountain House was torn down in the 1960s. Wentworth Hall closed its doors in 1971, and the Hawthorne Inn burned two years later. In the five years after *Yesterdays* was first published, two more of the most famous hotels succumbed: the Jackson Falls House was demolished in the late 1970s; the enormous Gray's Inn caught fire in 1983 and, in about forty-five minutes, was "flat to the ground," the director of the Historical Society recalls. Times looked grim.

Luckily, times changed. The beauties of the valley have begun to appeal anew, while the Jackson Ski Touring Foundation has built trails and encouraged smaller hotels to coax along the age of skis. Small old inns like the Inn at Thorn Hill have begun to revive;

today, two of Jackson's grandest Victorians, Wentworth Hall and the Eagle Mountain House, show signs of life.

Wentworth Hall is North Conway developer Mallett's second venture in rescuing such aging extravaganzas. His technique, paralleled by hoteliers elsewhere, is described in another updated phrase: the "condominium resort complex." Adding new structures on the grounds and dividing the hotel itself into units for sale, Mallett and others have found a way to revive such holdovers. Where many developers have ruined much of the beauty of the setting in the process, Mallett has kept much of the grounds intact at Wentworth Hall.

Resort meant more than bed and breakfast to the nineteenth century. It meant a total way of life that required a total environment. The 1880s Queen Anne main buildings of Wentworth Hall, which still overlook the falls of the Wildcat River, occupied only a portion of the acreage, which included a golf course, hiking trails, bridle paths, vegetable and flower gardens, barns, a laundry, a print shop, telegraph offices, garages, shops, and clubhouses. Some thirty or forty structures shaped a total lifestyle to satisfy the nineteen-century summer vacationers, who arrived by train and explored the surroundings on foot.

Today's clients, given mobility by their cars, head outward to the shops, trails, and tournaments around. Today's hotel manager operates differently, too. Where Wentworth Hall, 1892, supplied and cared completely, producing fruits, vegetables, and flowers on the premises, Wentworth Hall, 1982, had more resources than it needed, more land and buildings than Mallett could, or cared to, maintain. "Uneconomic" or outmoded, they went down. In their stead, Mallett planted condominium vacation houses in clusters to share the amenities of the re-

In the nineteenth century, the beauties of Mount Washington brought countless tourists to local hotels. In the twentieth century, the nearby strip of Route 16—the "alley through the valley"—has earned this attraction the label Mount Eyesore.

stored hotel and finance its renovation. In the fall of 1983, ironically on the same day as the Gray's Inn fire, his "Wentworth Resort Hotel and Townhouse Condominiums" opened.

To preservationists, the $2 million rehabilitation-and-construction project went both well and badly. They score points against some demolition, against a certain slickness, and against the wall-to-wall posh of oversized couches and opulent "French Provincial." But they applaud the restoration of flagship buildings, the original materials and details on exteriors, the handsome awnings, potted plants, and other niceties. They recognize that the nineteenth-century leisure of walks to Jackson Falls must be supplemented by color television and cocktails by the pool.

The time-sharing system ("You own, we manage") may have the ring of Yuppie New England, but preservationists acknowledge that it helps to translate this Victorian resort hotel into the modern vernacular. Too trendy, some say. But most consider the fate of Gray's Inn and agree that for all the missing elements, Wentworth Hall endures.

Half a mile up the hill, a more piecemeal approach coaxed the Eagle Mountain House back to another sort of life. Kimball and Neysa Packard eked out improvements as they could. Unlike the Wentworth, the Eagle Mountain House land was already fractured: short-term owners in the 1970s had sold off the original seven hundred acres. Fifteen acres belonged to the hotel; another fifty, the golf course, were lodged in a conservation trust. So no condominium concoction financed with land sales could work. Bootstrapping did. Without big-scale bank accounts,

A picturesque swimming spot at Jackson Falls. What developers call a new vacation "vernacular"—a style of life—also depends on the pleasures of an older New Hampshire.

Wentworth Hall in its romantic past. Recently, the hall lost this front yard to a parking lot, but it gained stylish awnings, well-groomed grounds, and a second life.

they began to restore this place into a more homey enterprise. If sweat equity took its toll on the owners, it extended life for the inn.

Unlike Wentworth Hall, the Eagle Mountain House never closed. A shabby wraith, it loitered through the 1970s until the Packards found it. Ignoring the decay, the couple saw enchantment in the wide verandas overlooking the Wildcat Valley, in the grand dining rooms, and in the working hydraulic "birdcage" elevator. The Eagle Mountain House was structurally solid but worn and tacky. The 1950 ersatz-Victorian additions to the 1916 and 1927 decor made the lobby look like a K-Mart lighting showroom, Kim says. "Otherwise, everything was pretty much original." It also met modern code requirements. After a fire razed the original building in 1915, its replacement incorporated the area's first sprinkler system. In 1982, the Packards bought their elegant artifact.

For three years, the couple invested much money and limitless energy to restore the old hotel's former grandeur, drafting those who shared their vision. Typical of their hands-on, help-out style, Kim, Neysa and sixteen other staff members "pulled an all-nighter" to repaint the lobby ceiling the day before their opening on June 25, 1982. Bootstrapping, alas, is a fatiguing way of life. "It's a full-time job," says Neysa. "It's three times a full-time job." Worn out, the Packards sold out in 1985, but new buyers will carry on their work.

Meanwhile, the house breathes an air of renewed life. Three ceiling fans swing a stately circle where the offending forest of chandeliers once hung. Richly hued slipcovers cover the lolling bamboo chairs where guests play chess, chat, or sip coffee from a warming tray on the wicker table. "We built on the original concept," Kim says. "People didn't spend much time in their rooms at these places, they came and socialized in the main rooms." No television, no phones. Entertainment ("no rock, but the place lends itself to swing and folk") and elaborate menus court both a younger clientele and the old crowd. As the rockers stretch along the veranda above the trim lawn, the vision of other guests of summers past seem to join them. Hopefully, new guests in summers yet to come will confirm Eagle Mountain's second life.

Different in scale, approach, product, both these New Hampshire resorts evoke the past yet have adapted its charms for present needs. In so doing, they define the essence of historic preservation for all the splendid summer artifacts of New England today. Can they and their peers elsewhere contrive an afterlife? The question still haunts the country landscape.

The Eagle Mountain House, also in Jackson, sprawling its way into the late twentieth century.

The classic connected New England house and farm buildings on a dairy farm in Windsor, New Hampshire, were captured in this Depression-era photograph.

9. The Landscape of Farming: Rural New England

In 1855, Herman Melville wrote, "Save a potato field here and there at long intervals, the whole country is either in wood or pasture. As for farming as a regular vocation, there is not much of it here. At any rate, not many by that means accumulate a fortune from this thin and rocky soil, all whose arable parts have long since been nearly exhausted." *Exhausted, thin, rocky*—the adjectives could have been written on the wagons heading west from New England. And yet the region's farmland was, and is, richer

Asparagus gone to seed softens the already romantic look of a picket fence on a Harvard, Massachusetts, farm.

and more complex than the cliché. As early as the seventeenth century, Francis Higginson spoke of its patchwork nature. "Masthulets Bay" was a land "of divers and sundry sorts," he wrote. "At Charles River as fat black earth as can be seen anywhere, and in other places you have a clay soil, in other gravel, in other sandy." Now, as then, the look of the land is more a sign of its diversity than its impoverishment; the Yankee farmstead is at least as contrary as the stereotypical Yankee farmer. The fertile river valleys

nourish abundant crops, and even the stone-strewn hills grow not only the proverbial crop of rocks, but fine forage and the tangiest apples in America.

For many, the farm is the symbol of the region. The rolling fields, crosshatched by stone walls, are etched in the national imagination. So is the architecture: the farmhouse, the barn, the scraps of sheds and outbuildings. Together, they link hands like an extended family ("Big house, little house, back house, barn," goes the nursery rhyme). The lone tree poised against the pasture, the fields of tassel-topped corn, the grassy slopes nuzzled by cows, the meandering roads, and the rural hamlets bespeak an agrarian order, New England's spirit and soul.

For generations the farm has mirrored both the beauty and the erosion of that spirit; it has recorded alike the settlement and unsettlement of New England. From the Civil War on, the landscape registered the toll taken by mechanization and industrialization. As agriculture enlarged and tech-

nology changed, many of the region's scenic farms, picturesque and patchy, proved inhospitable to the new machinery. The lure of the mill, the pull of the West, claimed their owners. Families in the marginal hill country abandoned their bankrupt farms. "Steadily the river valleys, rich in water power, are robbing the uplands of their population," an observer mourned in 1900. "The people of New England are running down hill. Massachusetts has built the factory and mortgaged the farm."

If the nineteenth century saw a decline in agriculture, the twentieth almost saw its demise. After World War II, the troubles became outright catastrophes. The rural exodus continued to rob the back country of its farmers; the urban exodus to the countryside brought city folk and suburban homes to occupy its best soil. In 1937, the *WPA Guide to Massachusetts* could still call Concord "the trading center for farm and garden products." Less than half a century later, the town of Emerson and Thoreau bedded more commuters than vegetables. Half an hour from Boston, Concord was emblematic: the state had lost

three-quarters of its two million farm acres.

So it went across the region. No matter that New England's remaining farms were blessed with superior soil, or that the growing cities needed their fresh produce; the fields still turned into plots for split-levels. Spring rains fell on asphalt, and Chevies parked where cows once grazed. For decades, new suburbanites covered acres of the landscape with tract housing while their streets, schools, and sewers raised taxes for farmers. Mark Kramer's *Three Farms* described the spiral of disaster in 1980: "Yankee farming today takes place in an atmosphere of siege. The banker is always at hand."

In less-populated corners, the siege was not a land squeeze but a land glut caused by hard times. In Maine, Vermont, and northern New Hampshire, forests consumed the abandoned countryside. Though less permanent than asphalt, the trees blotted out the farm landscape. "New England's stone walls now wander through woods rather than pastures," historian William Cronon recorded in *Changes in the Land.* Survey New England from the sky, says planner Wesley Ward, associate director for land conservation of the Massachusetts Trustees of Reservations: "The fields haven't sprouted houses. They've sprouted trees."

The progression from farmland back to idle soil is not ugly: first the daisies, goldenrod, and cockleburs come to color the open fields; then the brush, scrub pine, and oak. Finally comes the gentle second growth of trees that now covers three-quarters of New England's land. Benign though the view is, in the end the woods have choked the landscape; the soil provides scant food for a region short of it. The pastoral landscape vanishes.

Saving Farmland for Farmers

A letter to the Massachusetts Department of Food and Agriculture from George Steere, a farmer in

The picturesques enclave of the Stillman farm in Lunenberg, Massachusetts, is kept from encroaching development by conservation restrictions.

Southwick, speaks louder than any graph of decline. "I am eighty-three years old," Steere wrote, "and I have no relatives that are interested in the farm, but I have a farmer who would buy it at a price." His letter went on to predict the familiar grim finale for the Southwick farm: "The real-estate developers have their eyes on it."

Five generations of Steeres had farmed the land, tending their homestead since 1795; the Connecticut River Valley earth nourished crops of potatoes and apples and a fine small herd of Guernsey cows, for George Steere and finally for his renting neighbors. They would indeed "buy it at a price." In the 1980s, however, the price was too high. George Steere's rolling land was prime for agriculture, but it was also prime for another "product": houses.

The THICKLY SETTLED road signs told the same sad story for two more aging Massachusetts farmers. In Lunenburg, the sun silvered the silos and painted a swath of yellow on the rolling 350 acres of the Stillman farm, but the traffic heading past the farmhouse, bound for the computer belt between Routes 128 and 495, was less bucolic. So, too, thirty miles away in Westborough, development threatened the Nourses' colonial farmstead. Though settled here for decades, these families faced the threat common to much of New England: the fertile land and splendid landscapes were worth more sold than seeded, more as housing tracts than as farms. Though the settings are idyllic and the houses historic, these farmers have all their equity in the land. None of them could afford to pass the family farm on to the next generation or to sell at a price another farmer could pay. Would the Stillman and Nourse heirs lose their chance to work their families' farms? Would developers grid the Steere acres into subdivisions?

In the case of these three vintage Massachusetts farms, the answer was no. The Bay State's tradition of open-space advocacy and an activist Commissioner of Agriculture named Frederic Winthrop, Jr., intervened to ease the farmers' plight. "Those who

leave their footsteps on farmland" are the best protection, Winthrop wrote. To help a farm, help a farmer. Massachusetts, like the rest of the region, had never zoned to save its good soil; it had no land-use plan to protect farmers. To fill this gap, Winthrop and others began to initiate programs to support farmers' labors.

In the 1970s, farm conservationists tackled the problem with a tax solution. As land values soared, based on their value as buildable real estate, farmers paid taxes as high as the developers'. To correct this inequity, the Commonwealth put through a 1974 constitutional amendment to tax farmland on its value as farmland rather than on its potential value as houselots. In Massachusetts and, eventually, throughout New England, the differential tax assessment took hold.

It was only a start. Tax adjustments were enough to keep some farmers farming, but how would the Steeres, the Stillmans, and the Nourses be able to pass the land on to the next generation? State purchase of development rights was the answer that evolved. Doggedly, Winthrop and his department pushed state politicians. Winning support from a succession of governors, the commissioner probed for mechanisms to retain farmland and hence the rural

landscape. Two years after the tax amendment and Winthrop's arrival, Massachusetts launched the first statewide plan to buy development rights from farmers. Paying farm owners the difference between the value of their land for development and its value as farmland, the Commonwealth secured the Agricultural Preservation Restriction (APR) in return: from now on, only farms may stand here. Housed in cramped city offices furnished with dusty philodendrons, the department's Bureau of Land Use led the region in this novel notion—paying farmers to keep their land as food plots, not houselots. By the mid-eighties, the legislature had voted to issue some $45 million worth of bonds for the program. With state and local aid, the bureau had closed deals on the first 120 farms, with another 75 en route: a total of twenty thousand precious acres.

To some supporters of the program, farmland was simply an amenity of open space; it was the scenic landscape of tourism, vistas that offered relief from the congested corridor of megalopolis. To others, it was part of an essential environmental and ecological network, a means of protecting aquifers and habitats. For all, farmland was a vital source of fresh produce —a food machine. With eighty-five cents of every food dollar leaving the region, and eighteen calories of fossil-fuel energy needed for every calorie of food brought in, that machine needed fixing. The APR program had few critics. "It was an idea whose time had come," said Tim Storrow, chief of the Bureau of Land Use.

Using the program, the Steeres, Stillmans, and Nourses have sold the development rights of their farms to the Commonwealth. Now they can afford to pass the land to younger farmers or leave it to their own families. Farm owner, farm buyer, farm renter benefit. Unfortunately, money for all this is short. The lines to sell are long. Neither zoning nor land protection has come of age, and the public cannot afford to buy every endangered acre. Still, Massachusetts has made a start.

The sense of stewardship in the state reflects not only its liberality but its density. "Massachusetts is in the forefront just because crowded conditions are here and the public sensitivity is here and the money is available," says Douglas Wheeler, former head of the American Farmland Trust. Though the state has not marshaled a total land-use plan, the only true safeguard, it has inventoried its landscape to suggest which farmlands must remain intact. Second on the farm preservation front in New England, says Wheeler, is Connecticut, where "they are down in some cases to the last few farms." Here, in the southern tier of New England, the proximity and population of New York have made the situation even more desperate. "Connecticut had been losing farmland more than any other state," Mary E. Goodhouse, executive assistant to the commissioner in the state's Department of Agriculture, observes: in 1880, 80 percent of the state was devoted to agriculture; in 1974, 16 percent. Today, Connecticut's farmland values stand third in the nation. "We're a very desirable place to live," Goodhouse says. "A lot of business and industry is here, and just about every corner is in danger of being developed into residences."

Maintaining such idyllic New England landscapes as this pasture in Tunbridge, Vermont, is the goal of conservationists.

To barricade its farms from the wall-to-wall houses and sprawling corporate boxes, Connecticut, too, began to lower farmland taxes as early as 1963; fifteen years later, it, too, launched a development-rights purchase program. In the next five years, the state paid more than $8 million for five thousand acres on eighteen farms. More than two hundred fifty applications backload the commissioner's files, attesting to the lack of zoning or other protection. Yet, if commercial threats mount, so does the urge to create "farmland forever."

Guardianship has come more slowly in the other four New England states. Despite predictions by the U.S. Soil Conservation Service that Rhode Island's few farms would vanish by the year 2000, a development-rights plan voted in 1982 has been stalled. New Hampshire's full-speed-ahead growth mentality has undercut protection measures on the books in that state. Maine's poverty and far slower pace have led to similar inaction. And, for all Vermont's sensitivity to environmental issues, public mechanisms have done little to stop an avalanche of suburban homes and Alpine ski resorts in this most agricultural state.

In Land We Trust

Scenic or not, Vermont's landscape of thirty-four hundred dairy farms suffers severely from the distress of the dairy industry as a whole. Add to that the pressure of suburban development and recreational growth. Fearful of the onslaught, Vermonters passed farmland-acquisition laws in 1970 and pioneered in environmental controls with Act 250 governing land use that same year. Neither approach could stop the vacationization and exurbanization of the countryside. The ski lodges swallowed Sugarbush. The high-tech hideaways and Executive Colonials spread through the fertile crescents of the Champlain and

Mad River Glen resort: the chairs are ghostlike reminders of the absent vacationers, whose impact worries Vermont farmers.

Connecticut River valleys at Burlington and Brattleboro. Farmers, tempted by the future worth of their soil for houselots, or worried about local reverberations, didn't touch the state's funds. The much-touted protection of Act 250 provided a process for review of land use but was less a naysayer than a "quality control over development," says conservationist and planner Rick Carbin. Neither helped. Farmland still disappeared.

As the pace quickened, so did concern. The Ottauquechee Land Trust set up shop in Woodstock, Vermont, and in 1980 opened a full-time office. Four years later, the private agency (which Carbin directs) had made fast some ten thousand of the state's six hundred thousand acres of prime farm acreage. Paying from $5,000 an acre in the sparse Northeast Kingdom to $50,000 on the tempting shores of Lake Champlain, Ottauquechee gathered more than fifty conservation easements. Money, credit backing, and donations of land came from family trusts and foundations, including such open space and ecology advocates as the Connecticut River Watershed Council or the Vermont chapter of the Nature Conservancy. Ottauquechee's conservationists ranged across the state staking the earth, farm by farm.

Occasionally, the procedure was a clockstopper operation: the down-to-the-wire purchase of the 350-acre Hartland farm left fifty minutes to spare before bank foreclosure. Usually, it was less frantic and more complex. When the suburban land rush invaded Brattleboro's 150-year-old Unaitis Farm, for instance, Ottauquechee was invited to counsel the town. Its planners showed the community how to buy the farm and lease it back to a farmer with an option to buy. Thinking beyond the lone site, Brattleboro also undertook a far more comprehensive farmland-planning effort to protect its agricultural resources.

"Sugarbush Valley Keeps the Heat On," read a headline in the Mad River *Valley Reporter*, recording another region under assault. The mountainside could "turn out to be a disaster visually," said a planning commission member in the same article. The Sugarbush spillover so alarmed Warren residents that a float in their annual Fourth of July parade featured a mock bulldozer ravaging the landscape, and the country store sold FOREVER FARMING T-shirts. When the real version of that bulldozer threatened the most scenic vista in the town, Warren officials, too, sought Ottauquechee's help.

If the Vermont farmscape is New England's most picturesque rural resource, Warren's 175-acre Elliott farm is the epitome of that calendar art. Covering three of the four quadrants at the crossroads above the town, the farm's billowing fields stretch to the mountains in a view of pastoral eloquence. Yet, for all

The bucolic landscape of Irasville, Vermont, is threatened by recreation seekers.

the landscape's lyricism, when its owners died, the fate of both farm and view looked dismal.

Standing at the crossroads, Harry Smith, a seventy-nine-year-old neighbor, scans the nearby store that used to be a one-room schoolhouse and surveys the larger scene. "Back years ago," says Smith, "there used to be seventy-six dairies. Now they're down to two." Charting the ownership of the four corners, Smith turns to face one farm field leased by a polo club. The club's presence is symbolic of the elite that both supports and menaces the preservation of the landscape—supports it through fees, menaces it by its presence—a presence that escalates prices and transforms farms into subdivisions. That kind of real-estate pressure might have spelled doom for the Elliott farm; the lack of zoning plus the ease of utility and sewer hookups might have meant clear sailing for the apostles of divide and parcel. Here, too, however, Ottauquechee began to promote the plow against the bulldozer. Acting as a real-estate broker, its farm advocates found a "conservation-minded owner" to buy one of the three corners of the crossroads. Their victory was not complete, however: this owner plans to build a few houses there. "Compromises always come into play," says Carbin. Nor is salvation guaranteed. Two corners remain for sale, and the question persists: Will the four corners that make the splendid vista stay an unsullied sight?

Natural beauty can't guarantee the farm landscape. Neither can architectural excellence or a long history. To preserve the farm heritage, even long-time museums have had to adopt alternate means. One such is a superlative Victorian estate, the Park-McCullough house in Bennington, Vermont. Enamored of the landscape, Trenor Park planted this

The carriage house and barns at the Park-McCullough mansion and farm in Bennington, Vermont.

opulent French Second Empire "summer cottage" on his father-in-law's farm in Bennington in 1865. Little more than a century later, Park's heirs, the McCullough family, equally devoted to site and structure, listed the complex on the National Register of Historic Places and turned it into a museum. Alas, the family could no longer afford to keep the adjacent farm. Recognizing that the 350-acre farm was essential to the historic context, they, too, turned to Ottauquechee.

In a time-consuming procedure, the conservationists assembled "a financial package for the family and for those who want to work it," in attorney Darby Bradley's words. The novel approach apportioned the farm and mansion grounds—some for sale to raise funds, some to farm—all with restrictions to preserve the whole. Life on the farm is still "tenuous," say Marc and Jeanne Huyle, the young couple who farm the land today; the future is not yet sure. Nonetheless, the panorama and the lingering complex of buildings give this landmark a true sense of history and underscore the point that saving the ensemble—scenic ambience, splendid architecture, and functioning farm—is imperative.

In Cummington, Massachusetts, at another beautiful and historic farm, the William Cullen Bryant homestead, the Trustees of Reservations have adopted new modes to secure "the rolling countryside where one of America's most beloved literary figures began his communion with nature." First, the

trustees restored the Old Homestead as a museum. Then, working more expansively, they leased its fields to farmers. Finally, to secure the larger landscape, the group—acting through its affiliate, the Massachusetts Farm and Conservation Land Trust (MFCLT)—bought three nearby parcels. Using the state's development-rights program to finance the purchase, they assembled enough land to guarantee the Old Homestead's long-term economic viability and protect its historic environment. Here and elsewhere, the MFCLT has brought a total of nineteen farmland parcels with 1,850 acres valued at $7,066,000 into the state's fold, consolidating similar farms to make them financially feasible. One by one, farm by farm, almost furrow by furrow, it is a process that tasks even the staunchest advocate. "Land-conservation work is time-consuming and expensive," Ottauquechee's *Quarterly Report* concedes.

Nonetheless, playing something of the role of the gentleman farmer of old, creative state and private conservation programs have become benefactors across New England. The Maine Coast Heritage Trust champions the coastal Laudholm farm in Wells, Maine; the Society for the Protection of New Hampshire Forests works to save farm and forest alike. Indeed, some sixty sources of support appear in the pages of the *New England Directory of Agricultural Land Retention.* From water-conservation departments, concerned with farmlands as aquifers, to agricultural extension programs, more and more agencies rally to put together pieces of the puzzle.

The Farmer's Footsteps

Pieces they are. For all parties recognize that land conservation alone cannot save rural New England's thirty thousand farmers on their far-flung five million acres. "Land-use regulations, Act 250, special taxation, may help, but it's still more profitable to develop the land," landscape architect Michael Smiley told the Lincoln Institute for Land Policy. "Cluster zoning, transfer of development rights—sure, you can save a good deal," he said. "But it's too expensive to hold on to the large scale." Making farming viable

The summer home of poet William Cullen Bryant—intact, courtesy of the Trustees of Reservations.

The view from the porch of the Bryant homestead has changed little over the decades. Credit for the preservation of the surroundings goes to the trustees who secured farmland along with the homestead itself to ensure both aesthetic harmony and economic survival.

Peacemeal Farm in Dixmont, Maine, where the Wil-coxes, who "always loved the country," took over a failing farm and made it live through organic farm-ing.

for "those who leave their footsteps" comes first.

Federal programs that aid mega-farmers elsewhere often hurt rather than help the miniature landscape of New England. "Show the federal administrators a machinery inventory that does not include a fifty-thousand-dollar combine, a fifteen-thousand-dollar truck, or at least a couple of thirty-thousand-dollar tractors, and their eyeballs begin to glaze over," says Byron Jones in *The Farming Game*. "Talk about improving the soil by plowing down clover instead of raising corn and they will have to be somewhere five minutes ago. After all, it takes no longer to write a million-dollar loan than it does one for ten thousand."

Still some see hope for New England's farmers, despite unsympathetic federal programs, competition for the land, high petrochemical prices, and the dilemmas posed by taxes, marketing, and distribution. New England's antiquity and so-called obsolescence could equip it for tomorrow, some feel. Citing geography, good soil, good climate, good rainfall, and proximity to a large market, *The Economic Prospects of Northeastern Agriculture* suggested that when it is profitable to be farming anywhere in the United States, it is even slightly more profitable in the Northeast. Small seems especially beautiful in "the diversified farming pattern, small size, and substantial off-farm earned income of New England farms," noted a Council for Northeast Economic Action report. Even the lack of processing facilities and efficient distribution may be overcome by "the Europeanization of our cities," as Paul Hawken of Erewhon Foods, a natural-foods chain, calls the urge to buy fresh, not processed, food.

"Massachusetts Grown and Fresher," "From New Hampshire Fields to New Hampshire Tables," "Vermont Seal of Quality." Such state slogans promoting locally grown produce reflect how the more aggressive farm bureaucrats seize on that spirit. Across the region, old-time agencies like the Grange or extension services have come of age. Some even join with the three-thousand-member Natural Organic Farmers in the twin-pronged quest for better markets and better ways to grow. Simultaneously, a new network of politicians and farm policymakers broaches issues from the specific to the super-scale: from chemicals that pollute groundwaters to transportation and marketing problems to national and international policies.

Meanwhile, the farmer in the field toils on. "The real hope," Wesley Ward notes, "lies in the farmers who are making a living. There are some very good young or middle-aged farmer-growers who are changing to meet the conditions and are doing well." In their skill lies the promise, he says; carefully husbanded farms and flexible, intelligent farmers provide the basis for survival. "It's no longer the backwater family farm," says Fred Schmidt, a University of Vermont professor and political aide in Washington, "but a dynamic growing part of American agriculture."

The New Agrarians

Ever since the back-to-the-earth sixties, the number of counterculture farmers and part-time farmers, of urban farmers and weekend-gardener farmers, has multiplied. Such "new" farmers are not new on the New England scene, of course. Even in the 1840s, Hawthorne wrote of Brook Farm's literary farmers heading back to the farm "with delectable visions of the spiritualization of labor." "Play farmers," Dallas Sharp called the turn-of-the-century part-timers, "digging among the rutabagas, playing the hose at night." Though similarly scorned by some "real" farmers now, the more tenacious "back-to-the-earth" New Englanders have fewer illusions and more blisters. Whether powered by what Lester R. Brown of World Watch calls an ethos of "conspicuous frugality" or seeking more traditional goals, they stabilize old farms and reverse old attitudes. Their vision, long lacking, often leads to innovation. An experimental farm, such as Cape Cod's New Alchemy may not alter farming methods soon, but its enthusiasm inspires. Experiments there may seem far from the

mainstream, yet so did compost heaps a few decades ago. "Organic farming and land trusts used to be wild, radical. You'd get cut off at the ankles," says Judith Gillan of the New England Small Farm Institute in Belchertown, Massachusetts. Contemporary philosopher-farmers from the Nearings to Noel Perrin go beyond the modest turf they plow to create trends and sympathies. Akin to the urban pioneers of a few decades ago, they publish endorsements of rural life that spread, touch the political realm, and ripple outward.

But the new agrarians do more than preach. Like the New England farmer of history, the new man or woman of the soil must scrape along in a kind of Yankee quick-step. Scrambling to survive, a couple may alternate tree farming with teaching, city skills with country habits. One member may draw a salary in computer technology, while the other works a one-acre garden and sells wood to neighbors and wool to a local weaving cooperative. Thus they stitch a patchwork of part-time work into a quilt of enterprises.

Take the Oshimas. In Pembroke, less than an hour from downtown Boston, Helen Oshima, a former biomedical researcher at Boston University Medical School, works twelve-hour days in season. Under her care, a seventeen-acre farm once turning to brush now offers a rich array of herbs. Sometimes aided by her husband, William Oshima, she produces two hundred organically grown varieties, for sachets, teas, and medicines. Her list runs from A (alkanet) to Y (yarrow) with such plants as perilla wood and teasel in between. The Trombe wall and solar greenhouse seem strange on the vintage farmhouse. But as observers everywhere report, farmers like Oshima help

Sheep raised by new-age herb farmer Helen Oshima. Returning the New England landscape to productivity, she has revived a former farm in Pembroke, Massachusetts.

preserve the land by infusing life and energy into once-fading farms. "There seems to be a continuing trend to smaller, more part-time farmers with other jobs," says Grace Gershuny of Vermont's Natural Organic Farmers, confirming the movement. They come, she says, "to lead a healthy life," to be independent, to make manifest their urge to help the fragile food chain.

Offspring and perpetuator of such attitudes, the Rural Education Center in Wilton, New Hampshire, sits in a splendid Federal mansion, its broad lawn strewn with random piles of wood to burn in its many fireplaces. Founded in 1979, the center, at Samuel Kaymen's Stonyfield Farm, spent five years training interns in rural skills. Preaching the need to rechart the total ecology, insisting that "a New England agriculture can be one of diversity and sophistication," the founding father both of the center and of Natural Organic Farmers advocates chucking out-of-state avocados for home-grown apples, and chemical fertilizers for compost heaps, thus stopping oil-dependency, and creating self-sufficiency.

In recent years, the center grounded this ideology in the commerce of a new enterprise—making yogurt. While establishment farmers have absorbed counterculture impulses, alternate farmers like those at Stonyfield have moved closer to the middle. As "non-profits we realized that we had to focus and pick our area—not how to grow food but how to get it out," says Gary Hirshberg, Kaymen's associate. Shifting from farming on the fringes to a marketing base, Stonyfield Yogurt has grown eightfold in two years; once sold in thirty local markets, it is now available in every major supermarket in New England. The region's farming is just as diverse, just as much of a patchwork as the landscape. Part-time farmers, farmer-entrepreneurs, age-old farmers—all share in saving New England.

Innovative thinking isn't limited to newcomers, however. The Appleton farm, New England's oldest, tempers new approaches with tradition as it reigns over the graceful Ipswich landscape a scant hour out of Boston. "East, West, Home's Best" looks out from over the fireplace, while a menagerie of cats, dogs, birds, and a parrot who does his level best to sound like a rooster convey a conventional sense of a farm. But the barn filled with test tubes and the scrapbook

Organic farming at Samuel Kaymen's Rural Education Center, which now brings a more entrepreneurial approach to its whole-earth ethos.

Appleton Farm in Ipswich, Massachusetts, enduring in its fourth century.

Appleton's herds are now used for scientific breeding.

on the "beefalo" (the cross between a cow and a buffalo bred there) show the updated attitude of the farm's owner, Joan E. Appleton.

The Appleton family history of public concern also endures in the gift of farm acreage to the Trustees of Reservations and in the hospitality extended to schoolchildren. "One of the few places where you can see people work," says Richard Margolis, former editor of *Rural America.* Here, life and death, work and play go on visibly, as they have for generations.

Another Appleton concern endures here too: that of improving agriculture. Comprising some eight hundred acres, the three-and-a-half-century-old farm survives on the use of its dairy herd for scientifically advanced breeding. In an era of mega-farms, no one would call the Appleton farm "one of the most commodious places in the country for cattle and tillage," as it was once described. Still, the mind-set that made Daniel Fuller Appleton exhibit his Jersey cow Eurotissima ("bred by himself, the world's record buttermaker of her day") at the Chicago World's Fair of 1893 still strikes visitors in the Appleton enterprise as they learn of the details of the scientific sperm-production program run by James Geigor or stare down the wary eye of the new Appleton beefalo. Above all, what endures on this New England farm is the spirit of enterprise, and especially the love of the farming life that is the hope for survival of all New England farms.

"There's a massive voice out there in New England saying 'we want to save the resource,' " landscape architect Michael Smiley puts it. Will that voice be heard? Will it undo the harvest of neglect? The answer is unknown. But its importance is acknowledged. For if New Englanders do listen, the rolling landscape that foliage-seekers call "scenic," the way of life census-takers call "rural," and the produce that food fans called "homegrown" may yet struggle into the twenty-first century.

The plight of dairy farming jeopardizes the scenic landscape in Vermont's North Kingdom.

10. The Natural Landscape: Habitats and Open Places

"Nature," writes Cape Cod naturalist Robert Finch, "is the largest object on my horizon." And yet there is no "natural" landscape in New England. The presence of the human hand is everywhere: in the dammed rivers and meandering stone walls, in the once-cleared fields abandoned to underbrush and the second-growth woodlands, in the farms and scenic roads. "Even in its origins the land was less virgin than widow," historian Robert Cronon writes.

Call it wilderness, outdoor heritage, open space, or environment, this countryside is New England's backdrop and boundary. The ragged coastline, the meadows and fields, the mountains and valleys, counterpoint the built-over cities and towns and have inspired the same sense of stewardship. "Even now we are breaking up the floor and wainscotting and the doors and the window frames of our dwellings to warm our bodies and seethe our pottage,"

The Appalachian Trail near Zealand Pond in the White Mountains, New Hampshire: the scenic wonders of an outdoors that is neither wild nor tame.

environmentalist George Perkins Marsh warned in 1854. Appalled by the excessive lumbering in his Green Mountains, Marsh sounded a call that would become prophecy. Citizens of the most densely populated region in America heeded it. With Emerson and Thoreau to guide them, New Englanders after the Civil War sallied forth from their sprawling cities on nature walks and summer vacations. To some, the sojourn was a mere "weekend habit," a romantic outing. "The great mass of nature lovers in the 19th century only seasoned their lives with nature," Peter J. Schmitt wrote in *Back to Nature*. To others, the contrast was enlightening. For, by the latter part of the century, there was precious little of the countryside left. The same frame of mind that created vast national parks in the unsettled West caused New Englanders to worry about their own "wilderness," and to work to conserve it. "The cradle

A vista of the Berkshires seen through the cultivated garden of the Naumkeag estate, preserved by the Trustees of Reservations.

The Charles River at Natick, shaped into a park and preserve half a century ago, reflects an environment both natural and man-made.

ing and has fostered an awareness of the threats to those holdings and the larger environment. From acid rain's insidious devastation to what the *Vermont Environmental Report* calls the "Coloradofication" of Vermont, the bruising of the countryside goes on. The landscape legacy, eroded by many hands, has never needed tending more.

The Longest Trail Awinding

Like so many of New England's natural preserves, its longest one, the Appalachian Trail, owes its existence to a citydweller, Benton MacKaye, and its endurance to a half-century of stewardship. MacKaye broached his plan to relieve the "dinosaur cities" in the *Journal of the American Institute of Architects* in 1921. "The Appalachian Trail: An Experiment in Regional Planning" argued for a wilderness footpath, as a reminder to East Coast residents that "the whole world was not a city." His "path to natural living" would link and widen existing trails and preserves, from the peak of the great Katahdin in Maine to Springer Mountain, Georgia. It was a work of two decades. The Appalachian Mountain Club, the Society for the Protection of New Hampshire Forests, and outdoor advocates from the Green Mountain Club to the Dartmouth College Outing Club had already secured segments of what would become the trail. Individuals had helped, too. "I said to myself [Katahdin] should belong to Maine," declared Percival Baxter. Governor of Maine, Baxter conserved and donated much of Katahdin and today's Baxter State Park. The 5,267-foot lord of Maine would eventually stand as the peak of MacKaye's trail. By 1933, the Appalachian Trail stretched 2,059 miles.

Even in MacKaye's day, encroachments marred the trail. The planner's "primeval barrier from eastern urbanization" crossed ridges, dipped into valleys,

of American ornithology," Roger Tory Peterson called Cambridge, where, in 1876, the Nuttall Ornithological Club became the Audubon Society. In turn, the Audubon Society, the Appalachian Mountain Club, and other groups came to the aid of the outdoors.

Charles Eliot—planner, Olmsted disciple, and Appalachian Club officer—posed the crucial question for them: "How can we add roads, or large buildings to natural landscape without destroying the very thing in search of which we left the city?" In 1891, Eliot proposed a system of public reservations—part park, part nature conserve—a Metropolitan Plan (later the Metropolitan District Commission) that would set aside fifteen thousand acres of park and reservation within twelve miles of Boston's State House in less than two decades. He also founded a private group, the Trustees of Public Reservations, to collect still more of the scenic landscape in the state.

Yet the question Eliot addressed is still alive in this compacted region where space is so scarce that it must be created. The century after Eliot has brought a landscape of mountains and valleys, forests and meadows, wetlands and coastal zones into safekeep-

interlaced with ancient roads—and, inevitably, collided with people. As time passed, the collisions multiplied. Roads through mountain valleys became highways; natural landscapes served as second-home sites; country stores and inns fell for fast-food, motel-filled strips. People were "loving wilderness to death," historian Roderick Nash observed. Exploitation by short-term users, erosion, wear, and litter marred the trail. So did commercialization and logging. Winding through the most populous section of America, the so-called people's trail was overpopulated, and the land around it was gradually being covered with asphalt. Bothered by more and more hikers, homeowners along the trail began to shoo them off their private ways.

Fortunately, one of the longest footpaths in the world is cherished by one of the largest conservation constituencies. The Appalachian Trail Conference, organized more than half a century ago, has sixty-five clubs, an amazing league of volunteer and professional caretakers. The thirty-thousand-member Appalachian Mountain Club (AMC) alone cares for three hundred miles of trail. In a rare partnership with state and national agencies, its volunteers pick up litter, blaze paths, and monitor the logging and dumping that might undo the trail.

With the backing of such a constituency, Congress voted to tuck the Appalachian Trail into the National Trail System Act in 1968 and, ten years later, began to fund purchases of land around the path. Today the Park Service has bought land to guarantee a natural border to the trail and has relocated it from private to public property. In the process, it has pieced together everything from a "gentleman's farm" of less than an acre in Sherman, Connecticut, to portions of the Mahoosuc Range in New Hampshire. "One of the

The Long Trail in Vermont, established in 1910, pre-dated and joined the Appalachian Trail.

A bronze plaque in the State House at Augusta, Maine, commemorates Governor Percival Baxter's two-hundred-thousand-acre gift of a "shrine of wild natural beauty," Mount Katahdin, the northern peak of the Appalachian Trail.

most significant protection programs that has ever taken place in New England," says Steven Golden of the Park Service's Appalachian Trail Project office. At length, with more than twelve hundred individual segments secured, the Park Service claims it is "down to the tough cases" and will soon complete the work of securing the walkers' trip back to nature.

Meanwhile, though, environmentalists know that "nature" is not so simple to pin down for eternity. The Appalachian Trail, like all of New England's wilderness, forests, lakes, and wild animals, faces a more pervasive threat. Everywhere, the acid rain upwind from New England is causing environmental devastation. "In the past twenty years, over 60 percent of the softwood trees that grow at high elevations in the Appalachian Mountains have lost their foliage, died, or failed to reproduce," the Appalachian Mountain Club has warned. If one wishes "to preserve trees and life forms sustained by trees, there is no more time for paper shuffling," wrote John H. Mitchell, editor of the Audubon Society's magazine, *Sanctuary.* "Impending are many extinctions—of warblers, for example, and woodpeckers and wild turkeys, and [hawks], and ruffed grouse, and brook trout, and bears, and fishers, and bobcats, . . . and human beings?"

Guarding the natural environment of the urban Northeast clearly demands more than defending a narrow trail or handful of wilderness preserves from abuse. And, as the Reagan Administration weakens conservation measures, not only air pollution but the exploitation of natural resources for commercial needs has alarmed conservationists. From logging in the White Mountains to mining on Bald Mountain, Maine, environmental incursions are mounting.

The people problem cannot be dismissed. There are 340 people per square mile in New England (five

The red spruce, seen in this close-up of the west slope of Camels Hump, Vermont, shows the damage caused by acid rain and air pollution, which attack lakes, forests, and buildings in the region. Staking out parks and nature retreats is no longer enough to save the environment.

times the national average), and conservationists cannot open a preserve to the public without having to care for the crowds drawn to the attraction. The AMC has strained its resources to extend that care with great sensitivity.

Club members have even found themselves compelled to take on the role of building preservationists at one twenty-six-acre portion of the Appalachian Trail's Crawford Notch. Located in scenic splendor, the valley in the White Mountains in northern New Hampshire has long attracted crowds. Hence, when the historic Crawford House, located on a prize site, "mysteriously" caught fire and burned in 1977, the

land around it looked especially vulnerable. "Crawford Notch would probably have been bought by a developer, and there would have been condominiums or 'attractions,' " says Barbara Wagner, hut manager for the AMC. Instead, the club itself began to buy the land. Working with the Nature Conservancy and the Society for the Protection of New Hampshire Forests, the club raised money and purchased "the last remaining White Mountain Notch." Two years later, in 1980, they nominated the property, complete with its 1891 railroad station, to the National Register of Historic Places. Aided by a $75,000 grant from the National Park Service, the conservationists

This 1914 hut at Crawford Notch near Gorham, New Hampshire, is part of the Appalachian Mountain Club's hut system.

The Crawford depot restored by the Appalachian Mountain Club as a visitors' center cares for crowds with minimum damage to the environment.

restored the station. Today, the Crawford Notch depot serves as a visitor center, a jewel at the base of the mountains; and the AMC's outdoor advocates find themselves guarding the built and natural landscape alike. The costly fixup combined with ever-larger crowds severely taxes the resources of even this most established conservation group, but the new alliance has saved "probably the most historic site in the White Mountains," and one of the most splendid.

Wilderness in Retreat

Unfortunately, such a combination of preservation and conservation efforts doesn't always suffice. The arrival of tourists can wreak havoc with the place that draws them; nowhere is this more visible than in the wilderness park on Mount Desert Island, Maine.

What is today Acadia National Park began as the retreat to end all retreats. "Mount Desert is a jolly place, twenty miles long, ten broad; mountains in the middle; eight lakes between them; sea wall all around the island, sometimes five feet high, sometimes eight hundred," a nineteenth-century observer wrote. "Lots of caves full of pools; pools full of anemones. Surf breaks over said rocks considerably." Frederick Church and William Morris Hunt painted there. Artists and bohemians flocked to its wilderness, sleeping on corn-husk mattresses and waking with the birds. By the end of the Civil War, the cottages of the elite had "civilized" nearby Bar Harbor, and as the middle class joined them on the steamers from Boston, the sense of the town "passed from a field to that of a full-fledged spa," one historian

wrote. As the century advanced, lumberers and developers drew near.

Fortunately, another urbanite, George B. Dorr, was also on hand. The patrician Cambridge vacationer and relative of horticulturalist Charles Sprague Sargent responded to the threat of "scenic mayhem" and "ruthless spoliation" voiced by that other Cantabrigian, landscape architect Charles Eliot. Prodded by Eliot's father, president of Harvard, Dorr championed the first crusade for Acadia and set up a trust modeled on the younger Eliot's Trustees of Public Reservations. Using funds of his own and his friends', Dorr powered the drive and saved the land. When local developers tried to annul the trust, members gave the land, "nature's work of art," to the federal government: Acadia National Park was born.

So was the danger to it. By the 1980s, not much more than a century after its discovery, four million visitors a year were coming to the 38,000-acre pre-

Drawn by the beauties of Mount Desert Island, visitors in the 1880s began to fill the site with cottages (seen here). A hundred years later, a less appealing sprawl menaces one of Maine's most scenic coasts.

The Loop Road at Acadia, where visitors take in the coastline of Mount Desert, and the famous Schooner Head lookout, where nine condominiums destroy the natural view.

serve: the "primitive" Mount Desert Island held the second-most-visited national park in America. But as visitors soon found, the rest of the coast of rock and spruce and ocean-battered shore was not invincible to the attack of divide-and-conquer developers. Less than an eighth of Mount Desert's shore actually belonged to the public, and, at the prime wilderness outlook owned by the park, it began to show.

By the summer of 1985, a "subdivision" of nine vacation homes stretched across the rocky outcrop there. Dominating the formerly natural view of Schooner Head, the chief vista, they usurped the essence of the Acadia experience. Along the twenty-four-mile Park Loop Road, much of the coast stayed as unsullied as the land seen from the explorers' ships centuries ago. But the attack on the park's most dramatic vista clearly showed the wave of condominiums to come. The clutter of those second homes is unlikely to stop. "What's to prevent a Holiday Inn from coming in and building a development there?" Carrol Schell of the Park Service asks. "There's no question that whatever shorefront the park doesn't hold will be developed swiftly," Davis Hartwell of the Maine Coast Heritage Trust confirms.

On a cool summer day, with the intrusive Schooner Head complex in mind, Hartwell sat in his Northeast Harbor office and unrolled a map that underscored how slim a slice of coastline the National Park really holds. The erratic pattern—here, public land; there, private turf—makes a patched terrain and impedes saving the coast. Despite plans and more plans to preserve the shoreline from development, the land remains unprotected. "The Acadia Affair," the *Bar Harbor Times* called the last twenty

"Oh, who owns the lake?" Maine campers sing. This remains the question now, just as it was two decades ago when this picture of East Boothbay from private turf was taken.

years of sparring for the shoreline. Despite their efforts, the planners' solution of prohibiting development by zoning has failed. "Local resistance"—townsfolk who wanted the revenue from the land and resented Park Service interference—has nullified conservation.

To combat the antipathy of natives and the impotence of public agencies, the fifteen-year-old Maine Coast Heritage Trust has taken on a new role, however. Funded to guard not only the scenic splendor of the shore but its ecological value, the private conservation group saw Acadia as a focus for its larger coastal concerns. "Ecologically, the Maine coast is the meeting place for an array of terrestrial and marine ecosystems," a trust statement begins. It is "a place where spruce and fir of the great boreal forest grow side by side with hardwood species of southern woodlands, where strong tides flood vast intertidal areas twice each day, where sea birds share the Atlantic flyway with song birds of woodland and meadow." Scattered incursions, houses, hotels, parking lots on such crucial points as Schooner Head destroy both the chain of life and the natural landscape of New England. Protector of some twenty thousand acres through easement and acquisition, the trust seeks to fill in the interrupted park landscape.

"Bar Harbor is just one of those places that becomes a crucible," says Hartwell. With the Park Service prohibited from purchasing land at Acadia, the trust has played broker between the sellers and donors and the service. It has thus far negotiated more than one hundred easements to preserve the coast and hence maintain the landscape of Acadia.

"Why should not we who have renounced the King's authority, have our national preserves, where no villages need be destroyed, in which the bear and the panther . . . may still exist, and not be civilized off the face of the earth?" another conservationist asked in 1864. The eloquent polemic of Thoreau's *The Maine Woods* might serve as Acadia's insignia.

Island Real Estate

PRESERVE LIKE THE DICKENS. The bumper sticker pinned to the bulletin board of the Nature Conservancy's Boston office is the slogan of another crucible island. The Dickens-Lewis farm on Block Island, Rhode Island, with its undulating grasslands and "hollows" sweeping above a mile of rugged coastal bluffs, is a pastoral wetland as haunting as any in New England, especially in the late days of October, when the burning bush of autumn consumes the yellow stone walls, and the fading skies blur into the ocean. "We can be ethical only in relation to something we can see, feel, understand, love or otherwise have faith in," Aldo Leopold wrote in his *Sand County Almanac*. The crusade engendered by the Dickens-Lewis farm proves yet again how visual beauty can power the environmental movement.

Block Island is also a literal refuge, a way station for some 275 species of birds. "One of the three most spectacular birding spots in North America," in the words of the Rhode Island Audubon Society, as well as home for flowers like the Maryland golden aster and the rockrose. Despite an environment that has all these elements deserving of protection—vistas, wetlands, bird havens, rare wildflowers—it took one of New England's most concerted conservation efforts and more than a million dollars to ward off development and retain the Dickens-Lewis site.

The crusade for the Dickens-Lewis farm began more than a decade ago. "The very first thing that was saved was the core of Rodman's Hollow," says Keith Lewis, the bearded seagoing son of the man who launched the rescue. Driving his van across the quiet island to the farm, Lewis tells how his father, John Rob Lewis, began the Block Island Conservancy in 1972. Twelve years later, the local group had secured five preserves and, equally to the point, had aroused local enthusiasm. By the time the future of the Dickens-Lewis farm was threatened by its sale, the mechanism to save it was in place.

"There is a very strong interest on the island in

A summer house at Indian Head. Block Island is still spared the deluge of tourists that crowd island retreats like Nantucket and Martha's Vineyard.

saving the land," says Eve Endicott, field director here for the national Nature Conservancy. "They look at Nantucket and Martha's Vineyard and see what's happened there." If the market forces threatening Block Island were major, so was the will to save this piece of it. Endless labors—direct mail fundraising, meetings with the local community, publicity—aided the Block Island Conservancy. By 1985, the farm itself was secured.

But that was not enough. To retain the surroundings that give the Dickens-Lewis farm its sense of peace and to ensure its survival as a place for hikers and swimmers, the land nearby still needed saving. In concert with the local community, the national Nature Conservancy acted again. Working jointly with the town, the state, and foundations, national and local conservancies raised money to save the remainder of neighboring Rodman's Hollow's 180 acres.

Conservation proceeds apace elsewhere on the Island, too. Some $500,000 from a town open-space bond issue, plus $100,000 from the Block Island Conservancy, bought Mansion Beach, for instance; and in the decade since 1975, conservationists have doubled their holdings from 5 to 10 percent of the island. Unfortunately, prices have also doubled, and with them the danger to the island's open space. Like countless towns not zoned to control growth, Block Island is on the block.

"If land is not held by federal, state, or local governments, or private trusts, it will be developed," Esther Snyder, executive director of the Association for the Preservation of Cape Cod, says flatly. In Cape Cod's Barnstable County, the fastest-growing county in New England, the sought-after coastal landscape

The Mansion Beach property with a view of the Littlefield farm: bucolic grace saved by conservationists.

vanishes even faster than on island retreats. Even further out, that haven of nature, the Cape Cod National Seashore, established in 1961, draws five million visitors a summer. "The Cape's economy is its environment," says Snyder, but those who settle or despoil it forget that. Four thousand new houses a year bring a glut of problems from traffic to destruction of the limited groundwater supply. The pressure to commercialize such seaside land is interminable, open space finite, and the price to protect it high. Who can afford to buy and save this last landscape?

In Nantucket, where some three hundred licensed real-estate agents work for development, planners evolved one solution. Faced with three hundred new homes per year and 750,000 visitors each summer on the compact island, county planners watched oceanfront land vanishing. Of seventy miles of beach, only one and a half were truly open. Although "everyone has the run of the beaches," said William R. Klein, director of Nantucket's Planning and Economic Development Commission, "Nantucket is being bought out from underneath the Commonwealth." Squeezed by development, conservationists had already bought one-quarter of the fifty-square-mile island. It was not enough. So the planning commission devised another answer. In 1983, town meeting members voted 293 to 12 to pass the Nantucket Land Bank Bill. Within months, the law taxing each transaction of real estate at 2 percent was bringing in $40,000 a week that the commission could use to purchase open space—"beaches, wetlands, aquifer recharge acres, moorlands, heaths and any other lands which help to shape the settlement pattern of the community by promoting a village concept rather than a suburban sprawl."

Raising $1.6 million the first year and now averaging more than $50,000 a week, the Nantucket Islands Land Bank program has saved 340 acres of fragile moorland and beachfront; borrowing $11 million through revenue bonds, program administrators plan to purchase still more. Not surprisingly, other towns from Freeport, Maine, to Martha's Vineyard and the congested Cape Cod peninsula have begun to consider similar land banks. The state of Massachusetts may also enact similar legislation. The notion that money from the speculative furor ravaging the shore can save it is appealing. "It might buy seventy acres of trail system in Chilmark," Tom Counter of the Vineyard Conservation Society mused. "It might buy a hundred beach lots in West Tisbury . . . development rights on $2.5 million worth of farmland . . . three and a half Girl Scout camps. . . ." Still, planner Klein, who started it all in Nantucket, advises caution. "It shouldn't be considered a panacea," he says. "It's one more tool in the toolbox of preservation."

Stitching the Patchwork

Tools there are aplenty, and, in fact, more and more New Englanders search out and wield them. While environmentalists get into the real-estate business, buying easements or whole parcels to counter the developers, polluters, and abusers, concerned citizens lobby for temporary bans to stop building or zoning to modify it. Everywhere, advocates fight to save the flora and fauna that constitute New England's heritage and to protect endangered species, raise their voices to stop toxic waste disposal and the ravages of snowmobiles and beach buggies.

Saving the natural environment remains as much a step-by-step process as protecting a whole neighborhood by holding fast to single historic structures. Take the problem of wetlands. Case by case, the filling of each bit of marshy landscape seems minor. "I can't give one major wetland issue," says Douglas Foy of the Conservation Law Foundation. "It's a lot

of little ones." For all the measures on the books, the abuses mount: a garage gets built, dark-of-night dumping clogs a tidal estuary, a new riverside restaurant hardtops a habitat, the curve of a major highway erases a bog. Without watchdogs, violators flout laws; their projects swallow life-supporting fragments.

At its best, though, the preservation of such fragments is an expanding effort: guarding a wetland enlarges to protecting a river, to nurturing a river basin, to supervising a complete river valley. The Merrimack River Watershed Council is one such border-crossing operation: "Massachusetts gets the river that it inherits from New Hampshire," says Nathan Tufts, president of the council. The twelve-hundred-member group covers a valley that extends 115 miles along the river, and caring inevitably becomes interdisciplinary. Running through everything from old industrial sites to rural landscapes, the Merrimack could be a metaphor for New England itself.

The guardianship of the Merrimack valley began little less than a decade ago. Learning of $900 million mandated by the Clean Water Act to clean up the river, citizens feared development would follow. In 1977, the council banded together to protect what it knew would become prize real estate—the borders of the river, from its mouth at Plum Island to its source in Franklin, New Hampshire. Businessmen and naturalists, electronics specialists and environmental educators, joined to create a Greenway Plan. A Nashua, New Hampshire, waste-water treatment plant, a rowing club, the telephone company, and the Grace Episcopal Church filled the membership list of the Merrimack River Watershed Council. "We were trying to maintain a balance," says Tufts, between urban and rural, mill and farm, between state needs and community ones, between open space and working sites, all the time watching the river. While the Merrimack has become so pure that salmon now

*Sand dunes at Plum Island, Massachusetts, protected
by federal ownership, offer rare public access to the
shrinking shoreline.*

A Federal house in the village of Merrimacport, built in the nineteenth century when the river was used as a highway. For the twentieth century, it is a bucolic backdrop and recreational amenity.

swim in its waters for the first time in a century, pollution ruins groundwater wells elsewhere, and sends citizens of the region to drink—and drain—its purified waters. It is an irony, but as deep a threat as development, and one as much in need of attention. "We pick our issues," says Tufts, and the list seems interminable—now water depletion, now industrial pollution. "It's an industrial valley, we have these milltowns, so we couldn't take a purely environmental view," says Tufts. On the other hand, he says, "We have our farms. There's still a lot of land."

Islands to save. Salmon to secure. The river as amenity. The river as workaday place. Saving Deer Island. Staging a regatta. *The River's Reach,* the title of the council's newspaper, suggests its scope.

But if the competition for the land and the water in the region is ever fiercer, so is the constituency armed to defend them. Private groups raise funds to preserve wildlife refuges or scenic trails by purchasing them. The National Park Service expands its holdings. Citizens' coalitions tackle a tristate water-shed. State governments wrestle with the effects of acid rain on their rivers and buildings, forests and statues. Together, they eke out appropriate land-use policies to stem the commercialization or over-development of city and countryside. And all the while, awareness grows and the realization comes:

The landscape called New England is a continuum, shading from urban to rural to wild. To protect it, preservationists and conservationists must learn from each other and work together. They must become allies as never before. Such a shared stewardship may not remake the world or call a halt to its defacement, but in this most critical period and place in time, it is essential. Touched by many hands in the past, healed and held by many more today, New England's matchless environment is under assault. It could succumb to greed and neglect, but it could also become a model of caring and cooperation for the future. The challenge is monumental, but New Englanders have risen to such challenges before. The choice is ours.

Regional Source Guide

Addresses

Connecticut

State Historic Preservation Officer
Connecticut Historical Commission
 59 South Prospect Street
 Hartford, Connecticut 06106
Connecticut Trust for Historic Preservation
 152 Temple Street
 New Haven, Connecticut 06510
Hartford Architecture Conservancy
 51 Wetherfield Avenue
 Hartford, Connecticut 06114
Mystic Seaport Museum
 Mystic, Connecticut 06355
New Haven Colony Historical Society
 114 Whitney Avenue
 New Haven, Connecticut 06510

Maine

State Historic Preservation Officer
Maine Historic Preservation Commission
 55 Capitol Street
 Augusta, Maine 04333
Greater Portland Landmarks
 165 State Street
 Portland, Maine 04101
Maine Citizens for Historic Preservation
 597 Main Street
 South Portland, Maine 04106
Maine Coast Heritage
 Summit Road
 Northeast Harbor, Maine 04662

Maine Historical Society
 485 Congress Street
 Portland, Maine 04101

Massachusetts

State Historic Preservation Officer
Massachusetts Historical Commission
 80 Boylston Street
 Boston, Massachusetts 02116
Conservation Law Foundation of New England, Inc.
 3 Joy Street
 Boston, Massachusetts 02108
Essex Institute
 132 Essex Street
 Salem, Massachusetts 01970
Historic Massachusetts, Inc.
 80 Boylston Street, Suite 330
 Boston, Massachusetts 02116
Massachusetts Alliance of Preservation Commissions
 One Government Center
 Fall River, Massachusetts 02722
Merrimac River Watershed Council
 694 Main Street
 West Newbury, Massachusetts 01985
Plimoth Plantation
 Box 1620
 Plymouth, Massachusetts 02360
Preservation Studies Program
Boston University
 226 Bay State Road
 Boston, Massachusetts 02215
Public History Program
Northeastern University
 360 Huntington Street
 Boston, Massachusetts 02115

Sprightly signs point out the options for travelers.
Which way will New England go?

Society for the Preservation of New England
  Antiquities
  141 Cambridge Street
  Boston, Massachusetts 02114
Trustees of Reservations
  572 Essex Street
  Beverly, Massachusetts 01915

New Hampshire

State Historic Preservation Officer
New Hampshire Historic Preservation Office
Department of Resources and Economic
  Development
  105 Loudon Road
  Box 856
  Concord, New Hampshire 03301
New Hampshire Association of Historic District
  Commissions
  121 Water Street
  Exeter, New Hampshire 03833
New Hampshire Historical Society
  30 Park Street
  Concord, New Hampshire 03301

Rhode Island

State Historic Preservation Office
Rhode Island Historical Preservation Commission
  150 Benefit Street
  Providence, Rhode Island 02903
American Studies Area
Roger Williams College
  Bristol, Rhode Island 02809
Preservation Society of Newport County
  118 Mill Street
  Newport, Rhode Island 02840
Providence Preservation Society
  24 Meeting Street
  Providence, Rhode Island 02903
Rhode Island Historical Society
  110 Benevolent Street
  Providence, Rhode Island 02906

Vermont

State Historic Preservation Officer
Vermont Division for Historic Preservation
Agency of Development and Community Affairs
  Montpelier, Vermont 05602
Historic Preservation Program
University of Vermont
  Wheeler House
  442 Main Street
  Burlington, Vermont 08405
Preservation Trust of Vermont
  104 Church Street
  Burlington, Vermont 05401

Books

Adams, Henry. *The Education of Henry Adams.* Boston: Houghton Mifflin, 1973.

Antin, Mary. *The Promised Land.* Boston: Houghton Mifflin, 1969.

Beard, Frank A., and Bette A. Smith. *Maine's Historic Places.* Camden, Me.: Down East, 1982.

Bentley, William. *Diary, 1748–1819,* 4 vols. Salem, Mass.: Peter Smith, 1905–1914.

Berry, Wendell. *The Unsettling of America.* New York: Avon, 1972.

Beston, Henry. *The Outermost House.* New York: Viking, 1928.

Binford, Henry C. *The First Suburbs.* Chicago: University of Chicago Press, 1985.

Bridenbaugh, Carl. *Cities in Revolt: Urban Life in America, 1743–1776.* New York: Knopf, 1955.

———. *Cities in the Wilderness: The First Century of Urban Life in America, 1625–1742.* New York: Knopf, 1955.

Brooks, Van Wyck. *The Flowering of New England, 1815–1865.* New York: Dutton, 1936.

———. *New England: Indian Summer.* New York: Dutton, 1965.

A statue languishing at the Codman house before it was restored by the Society for the Preservation of New England Antiquities.

Bunting, Bainbridge. *Houses of Boston's Back Bay.* Cambridge, Mass.: Harvard University Press, 1967.

Burchard, John, and Albert Bush-Brown. *The Architecture of America: A Social and Cultural History.* Boston: Little, Brown, 1961.

Cambridge Historical Commission. *Survey of Architectural History in Cambridge,* Nos. 1–5. Cambridge, Mass.: MIT Press, 1966–1977.

Carson, Rachel. *Silent Spring.* Boston: Houghton Mifflin, 1962.

Ciucci, Georgio. *The American City: From the Civil War to the New Deal.* Cambridge, Mass.: MIT Press, 1983.

Commoner, Barry. *The Closing Circle.* New York: Knopf, 1972.

Costonis, John J. *Space Adrift: Landmark Preservation and the Marketplace.* Chicago: University of Illinois Press, 1974.

Cranz, Galen. *The Politics of Park Design.* Cambridge, Mass.: MIT Press, 1982.

Cronon, William. *Changes in the Land: Indians, Colonists, and the Ecology of New England.* New York: Hill and Wang, 1983.

Cummings, Abbott Lowell. *The Framed Houses of Massachusetts Bay.* Cambridge, Mass.: Harvard University Press, 1979.

Dubos, René. *The Wooing of Earth: New Perspectives on Man's Use of Nature.* New York: Scribner, 1980.

Dunwell, Steve. *Run of the Mill.* Boston: Godine, 1978.

Ehrlich, Paul. *The Population Bomb.* New York: Ballantine, 1983.

Ehrlich, Paul, and Ann Ehrlich. *Extinction.* New York: Random, 1981.

Eliot, Charles William. *Charles Eliot, Landscape Architect.* New York: Arno, 1972. (Reprint of 1902 edition.)

Finch, Robert, *Common Ground.* Boston: Godine, 1981.

Fitch, James Marston. *American Building: The Historical Forces That Shaped It.* Boston: Houghton Mifflin, 1947.

Fleming, Ronald Lee, and Lauri A. Halderman. *On Common Ground,* Cambridge, Mass.: Harvard Common Press, 1982.

Fox, Stephen. *John Muir and His Legacy: The American Conservation Movement.* Boston: Little, Brown, 1981.

Gans, Herbert. *The Urban Villagers.* New York: Free Press, 1962.

Glaab, Charles Nelson, and A. Theodore Brown. *A History of Urban America.* New York: Macmillan, 1967.

Gowans, Alan. *Images of American Living: Four Centuries of Architecture and Furniture as Cultural Expression.* Philadelphia: Lippincott, 1964.

Hale, Nancy. *New England Discovery: A Personal View.* New York: Coward, 1963.

Hamlin, Talbot. *Greek Revival Architecture in America.* New York: Dover, 1944.

Handlin, David P. *The American Home.* Boston: Little, Brown, 1979.

Hardin, Garrett, and John Baden. *Managing the Commons.* San Francisco: W. H. Freeman, 1977.

Hareven, Tamara, and Randolph Langenbach.

Glistening white spire on the 1792 meeting house in Center Sandwich, New Hampshire.

Amoskeag: Life and Work in an American Factory-City. New York: Pantheon, 1978.

Harrell, Pauline Chase, Charlotte Moulton Chase, and Richard M. Chase. *Arrowhead Farm: Three Hundred Years of New England Husbandry and Cooking.* Woodstock, Vt.: Countryman, 1984.

Harvard College Library, Dept. of Graphic Arts. *H.H. Richardson and His Office.* Cambridge, Mass.: Harvard University Press, 1974.

Hosmer, Charles B., Jr. *Preservation Comes of Age: From Williamsburg to the National Trust, 1926–1949,* 2 vols. Charlottesville: University Press of Virginia, 1981.

Jackson, John Brinckerhoff. *American Space.* New York: Norton, 1972.

———. *Landscapes,* Amherst: University of Massachusetts Press, 1970.

———. *The Necessity for Ruins.* Amherst: University of Massachusetts Press, 1980.

———. *Discovering the Vernacular Landscape.* New Haven: Yale University Press, 1984.

Jacobs, Jane. *Death and Life of Great American Cities.* New York: Random, 1961.

Jones, Bryan. *The Farming Game.* Lincoln: University of Nebraska Press, 1982.

Jorgensen, Neil. *A Guide to the New England Landscape.* Boston: Globe Pequot, 1977.

Kay, Jane Holtz. *Lost Boston.* Boston: Houghton Mifflin, 1980.

———. Introduction to *The WPA Guide to Massachusetts.* New York: Pantheon, 1983.

Kimball, Fiske. *Domestic Architecture of the American Colonies and of the Early Republic.* New York: Dover, 1966.

Kirker, Harold, and James Kirker. *Bulfinch's Boston, 1787–1817.* New York: Oxford University Press, 1964.

Kramer, Mark. *Three Farms.* Boston: Little, Brown, 1979.

Lears, T.J. Jackson. *No Place of Grace.* New York: Pantheon, 1981.

Leopold, Aldo. *A Sand County Almanac.* New York: Oxford University Press, 1966.

Lingeman, Richard R. *Small Town America.* New York: Putnam, 1980.

Lottman, Herbert R. *How Cities Are Saved.* New York: Universe, 1976.

Lynch, Kevin. *Image of the City.* Cambridge, Mass.: MIT Press, 1960.

———. *What Time Is This Place?* Cambridge, Mass.: MIT Press, 1972.

Marquand, John Phillips. *The Late George Apley.* Boston: Little, Brown, 1937.

Marsh, George Perkins. *Man and Nature.* Cambridge, Mass.: Harvard University Press, 1965.

Morris, David. *Self-Reliant Cities.* San Francisco: Sierra, 1982.

Mumford, Lewis. *The City in History.* New York: Harcourt Brace, 1961.

Nash, Roderick. *Wilderness and the American Mind.* New Haven: Yale University Press, 1982.

National Trust for Historic Presevation. *With Heritage So Rich.* Washington, D.C.: Preservation, 1983.

——. *Preservation: Toward an Ethic in the 1980s.* Washington D.C.: Preservation, 1980.

Old-Time New England: The Bulletin of the Society for the Preservation of New England Antiquities. Boston, 1910–present.

Peterson, Charles E., ed. *Building Early America.* Radnor, Pa.: Chilton, 1976.

Pierce, Neal R.. *The New England States.* New York: Norton, 1976.

Pierson, William Harvey, and William R. Jordy. *American Buildings and Their Architects.* vols. 1–4. Garden City, N.Y.: Doubleday, 1970–1978.

Primack, Mark. *Greater Boston Park and Recreaion Guide.* Boston: Globe Pequot, 1983.

Reps, John William. *The Making of Urban America: A History of City Planning in the United States.* Princeton: Princeton University Press, 1965.

Rifkind, Carole. *Main Street.* New York: Harper and Row, 1977.

Robinson, William F. *Abandoned New England.* Boston: New York Graphic Society, 1976.

Russell, Howard S. *The Long Deep Furrow.* Hanover, N.H.: University Press of New England, 1976.

Schumacher, E.F. *Small Is Beautiful: Economics as if People Mattered.* New York: Harper and Row, 1973.

Scott, Mel. *American City Planning Since 1890.* Los Angeles: University of California Press, 1969.

Scully, Vincent. *The Shingle Style Today.* New York: Braziller, 1974.

——. *American Architecture and Urbanism.* New York: Praeger, 1969.

Solomon, Barbara Miller. *Ancestors and Immigrants: A Changing New England Tradition.* Cambridge, Mass.: Harvard University Press, 1956.

Spirn, Anne Whiston. *The Granite Garden.* New York: Basic, 1984.

Stevenson, Elizabeth. *Park Maker: A Life of Frederick Law Olmsted.* New York: Macmillan, 1977.

Stilgoe, John R.. *Metropolitan Corridor.* New Haven: Yale University Press, 1983.

——. *Common Landscape of America, 1580–1845.* New Haven: Yale University Press. 1982.

Stobaugh, Robert, and Daniel Yergin. *Energy Future.* New York: Random, 1979.

Thoreau, Henry David. *Walden.* New York: Modern Library, 1981.

Thorndike, Joseph J., Jr. *Three Centuries of Notable American Architects.* New York: American Heritage, 1981.

Tolles, Bryant F., and Carolyn K. Tolles. *New Hampshire Architecture: An Illustrated Guide.* Hanover, N.H.: University Press of New England, 1979.

Tucci, Douglass Shand. *Built in Boston.* Boston: New York Graphic Society, 1978.

Udall, Stewart. *The Quiet Crisis.* New York: Holt, 1964.

Warner, Sam Bass. *Streetcar Suburbs: The Process of Growth in Boston, 1870–1900.* Cambridge, Mass.: Harvard University Press, 1962.

Whiffen, Marcus, and Fredrick Koeper. *American Architecture,* 2 vols. Cambridge, Mass.: MIT Press, 1981–1983.

Whyte, William H. *The Social Life of Small Urban Spaces.* Washington, D.C.: Conservation Foundation, 1980.

Zaitzevsky, Cynthia. *Frederick Law Olmsted and the Boston Park System.* Cambridge, Mass.: Harvard University Press, 1982.

Zube, Ervin H., and Margaret J. Zube, eds. *Changing Rural Landscapes.* Amherst: University of Massachusetts Press, 1977.

Picture Credits

I am indebted to the following individuals and institutions for permission to use photographs and other illustrations, in particular Frederica Matera and the Society for the Preservation of New England Antiquities (SPNEA):

Pages ii–iii Orland village, Maine: *Jane P. Gilbert.* vi Political map of the Eastern States: *from* Woodbridge's Geography, Boston, 1843. vii Gothic church: *Steve Rosenthal.* ix Italianate house; 1 White fence: *Frederica Matera.* **Prologue: page 2** Vermont leaves: *Frederica Matera.* 4 Trailers: *Willard Traub.* Tanks: *Frederica Matera.* 5 Covered bridge: *Frederica Matera.* 6 Concord view: *Boston Athenaeum.* 7 Charlestown highway ramps: *Peter Vandermark.* 8 Pebble Beach; Westpoint Village; 9 Mad River: *Frederica Matera.* 10 Gingerbread house: *Randolph Langenbach.* Belcourt Castle: *Frederica Matera.* 11 Barn: *Lee Nadel.* Lighthouse: *Thomas Hahn.* 12 Yale: *Frederica Matera.* 13 Abandoned house: *Chris Chadbourne.* 14 Hancock School; Lisbon School: *Frederica Matera.* **Part One: History: page 15** Three-hundredth-anniversary medal, Plymouth, Massachusetts: *SPNEA.* **1: The Building of New England: page 16** Plimoth Plantation: *Frederica Matera.* 17 Plymouth Rock monument: *SPNEA.* 19 Greenfield Common. *SPNEA.* 20 Parson Capen House: *Randolph Langenbach.* 22 Fairbanks House; 23 Leyden Street: *SPNEA.* 24 Hancock House: *Bostonian Society.* Salem's Chestnut Street: *SPNEA.* 25 First Congregational Church: *Frederica Matera.* Nickols-Sortwell House: *SPNEA.* 26 "Clock strikes twelve": *Smithsonian Institute.* Lowell girls: *University of Lowell.* 27 Cornwall Bridge depot: *Tom Zetterstrom.* 28 Morse-Libby Mansion: *SPNEA.* 29 Mark Twain House; Hartford cottage: *Thomas Hahn.* 30 Station House: *New Hampshire Historical Society.* 31 Gingerbread porch:

Muriel Mitchell. Vinland, Newport: *SPNEA.* 32 Charles River playground: *National Park Service.* Commonwealth Avenue: *Metropolitan District Commission.* 33 Art Deco diner: *Jane P. Gilbert.* 34 Church Court condominiums: *Steve Rosenthal.* 35 City Hall plaza: *Ezra Stoller.* **2. Preservation in New England: page 36** Obelisk at Concord: *Concord Free Public Library.* 37 Capital from mansion; 38 House of the Seven Gables: *SPNEA.* 39 Vassall-Longfellow House: *National Park Service.* 40 Deerfield's Old Indian House; Hancock Mansion broadside: *SPNEA.* 41 State House demolition: *New Haven Colony Historical Society.* 42 Old South Meeting House: *Bostonian Society.* Webb-Deane-Stevens complex: *Jackson Smith.* 43 Deerfield: *Emma Coleman, SPNEA.* 44 Ward House: *Essex Institute.* Nutting period portrait: *SPNEA.* 46 Appleton: *Florence Addison, SPNEA.* 47 Mystic Seaport: *Mary Ann Stets, Mystic Seaport Museum.* 48 Wolfe Tavern: *SPNEA.* 49 Acorn Street: *Frederica Matera.* 51 North End: *Jules Aarons.* 52 Atlantic Avenue: *Thomas Hahn.* 53 Touro Synagogue: *Newport Historical Society.* Gropius House: *Robert Damora.* 54 Bulfinch Court: *Blake Allison, Graham Gund Associates.* Royal River Brickyard: *Frederica Matera.* **Part Two: Saving the Town and Cityscape: page 55** Beacon Hill: *Bostonian Society.* **3. Waterfronts: Down to the Seashore and Riverside: page 56** Monhegan: *Randolph Langenbach.* 57 Figurehead; 58 Marblehead; 59 West River Marina: *Frederica Matera.* 60 1900 Harbor: *Rhode Island Historical Society.* 61 Stonington: *Judy Watts.* Nantucket street: *Nantucket Historical Association.* 63 Nantucket wharves: *Charles F. Young.* Siasconset fisherman's shack: *Linda Sussman.* 64 Twin beachhouses: *Venturi, Rauch, and Scott Brown.* 65 Fishing shack: *Janet K. Woodcock.* Commercial and T Wharves; 66 Faneuil Hall Marketplace: *Bostonian*

Society. 67 Quincy Market: *Steve Rosenthal.* 68 Chart House: *Randolph Langenbach.* 69 Commercial Wharf: *Frederica Matera.* 69 Mercantile Wharf buildings; 70 Fort Point Channel buildings; 71 Charlestown Navy Yard: *Steve Rosenthal.* 72 Ceres Street; 74 Workaday Portland; 75 Old Port Exchange: *Frederica Matera.* **4. Mills and Milltowns: Where Life Meets Work: page 76** Engineers at Merrimack Canal: *University of Lowell, Special Collections.* 77 Mill complex: *Randolph Langenbach.* 78 Factory housing; 79 Slater Mill: *Frederica Matera.* 80 Lawrence mills: *Jack Delano, Farm Security Administration.* 81 Clinton textile mill: *Wayne Soverns, Jr.* 82 Lower canal building: *Randolph Langenbach.* 84 Hildreth Building: Lowell Historical Society. 85 Mill atrium; Market Mills: *James Higgins, Lowell Historic Commission.* 86 Staircase; 87 Canal; 88 Lewiston's Main Street: *Frederica Matera.* 89 Lewiston mill; 90 Forge shop: *Randolph Langenbach.* 91 Pejetscot mill: *Jeanne Devereux.* 92 Lawrence: *Randolph Langenbach.* 93 Davol Square: *Gary Gilbert.* **5. Urban Neighborhoods: Preservation Begins at Home: page 94** Three-deckers: *Bob Rugo, Boston Redevelopment Authority.* 95 Brownstone stoops: *Frederica Matera.* 96 Porch, 1940s: *Fenno Jacobs, Farm Security Agency.* Roxbury porches: *Irene Shwachman.* 97 New Haven Historic District: *Frederica Matera.* 98 Starr Street before and after: *Thomas Hahn.* 99 Armory: *Frederica Matera;* Woods-Gerry House: *Rhode Island School of Design.* 100 George Prentice House; Dexter Avenue; 101 Benjamin Webber House: *Frederica Matera.* 102 1890 four-decker before and after: *Charles Sullivan, Cambridge Historical Commission.* 103 Chester Square: *SPNEA.* 105 Rutland Square (both): *Frederica Matera.* 107 Bridgeport's South End: *Bridgeport Public Library, Historical Collections.* 108 1887 John Howland House; 109 Seaside Park:

Frederica Matera. **6. Downtowns: Conserving the Core: page 110** Urban renewal: *Irene Shwachman.* **111** Washington Street: *Bostonian Society.* **112** Scollay Square: *Irene Shwachman.* **113** Old City Hall: *Architectural Heritage.* **114** Record-American Building; One Winthrop Square: *Childs, Bertman, and Tseckares.* **115** Quincy Market refurbished: *Steve Rosenthal.* **116** Batterymarch Building: *Alan Ward.* **117** Federal Reserve Bank; Proctor Building: *Robert Severy.* **118** One Exchange Place: *Frederica Matera.* **119** Newburyport's Inn Street: *Notter, Feingold, and Alexander.* **120** Newburyport market, mid-nineteenth century: *SPNEA.* **120** The market today; **121** Art Deco storefront; **122** Amesbury's Main Street; **123** Amesbury's Mill; **124** Main Street: *Frederica Matera.* **125** Chapel Street, 1890: *Willis N. Butricks, New Haven Colony Historical Society.* **126** Italianate building: *Frederica Matera.* **Part Three: Husbanding the Green Spaces: page 127** York farmers: *SPNEA.* **7. The Cultivated Landscape: Commons, Parks, and Parkways: page 128** Woodstock Common: *Woodstock Historical Society.* **129** Charles River promenade: *Metropolitan District Commission.* **130** Boston Common: *from Boston Miscellany, 1842, Bostonian Society.* **131** Washington elm: *Cambridge Historical Society.* **132** Keene Common (both); **133** House on Woodstock Common; Chelsea Common: *Frederica Matera.* **134** Royalston Common: *Randolph Langenbach.* **135** Litchfield Common: *Frederica Matera.* **136** Fens, Boston: *National Park Service.* **136** Benches in Kennedy Park; **137** Edgewood Park: *Frederica Matera.* Franklin Park: *Richard Heath, Franklin Park Coalition.* **138** Porch: *Frederica Matera.* **139** Bushnell Park, before: *Bushnell Park Foundation.* **140** Winged Victory, Bushnell Park: *Frederica Matera.* **142** Mt. Auburn Cemetery: *Cymie Payne.* **143** Old Granary Burial Ground: *Kenneth D.*

Mandl. **144** Gravestones, Marblehead: *Alan Ward.* **145** Merritt Parkway bridge: *Pamela Allara, State of Connecticut, Department of Transportation.* **8. The Landscape of Leisure: Estates and Resorts: page 146** Stoeckel Estate: *Tom Zetterstrom.* **147** Longyear Foundation: *Frederica Matera.* **148** Day Estate: *Steve Rosenthal.* Codman House: *Frederica Matera.* **149** Bowen House: *Alan Ward.* **150** Grande Allée, Crane Estate; **151** Crumbling Terrace; **152** Lyman House: *Frederica Matera.* **153** Rosecliff: *Preservation Society of Newport County.* **155** Hammersmith Farms: *Cymie Payne.* **156** Turrets: *Bar Harbor Historical Society.* **157** Bay View Inn (both): *Frederica Matera.* **158** Poland Spring (both): *SPNEA.* **159** Walloomsac Inn; **160** Holderness Inn; General store; **161** Norumbega; **162** Stonehurst; **163** Mount Washington's alley; Jackson Falls; **164** Wentworth awnings: *Frederica Matera.* **164** Wentworth Hall: *Randolph Langenbach.* **165** Eagle Mountain House: *Frederica Matera.* **9. The Landscape of Farming: Rural New England: page 166** Windsor dairy farm: *Jack Delano, Farm Security Administration.* **167** Harvard farm: *Mary Nadel.* **168** Graysville farm: *Farm Security Administration.* **169** Stillman farm; **170** Nourse farm: *Frederica Matera.* **171** Pasture, Tunbridge: *Suzanne Dworsky.* **171** Mad River Glen; **172** Moretown landscape; **173** Park-McCullough carriage house; and barns; **174** William Cullen Bryant Home: *Frederica Matera.* **175** Porch of Bryant Home: *Loring Conant, Trustees of Reservations.* **176** Peacemeal Farm: *Jane P. Gilbert.* **178** Nancy Jack Todd: *Lee Nadel.* Oshima farm: *Frederica Matera.* **179** Rural Education Center: *D. Burger, Stonyfield Farms.* **180** Appleton Farms; Appleton cows: *Frederica Matera.* **181** Vermont's North Kingdom: *Peter Vandermark.* **10. The Natural Landscape: Habitats and Open Places: page 182** Naumkeag Estate: *Alan Ward.* **183** Xea-

land Pond: *Edward Monnelly, Appalachian Mountain Club.* **184** Charles River, Natick; **185** Long Trail: *Frederica Matera.* **186** Bronze plaque: *Austin H. Wilkins.* Red Spruce: *John H. Mitchell.* **187** Mount Garfield. *G. Bellerose, Appalachian Mountain Club.* **188** Crawford Notch hut: *Appalachian Mountain Club.* **189** Crawford depot: *Frederica Matera.* **190** Mount Desert Island, 1880s: *Charles Pollock, SPNEA.* **191** Loop Road, Acadia; Schooner Head lookout: *Frederica Matera.* **192** East Boothbay: *John McKee.* **194** Summer house, Indian Head; **195** Dickens-Lewis Farm; Mansion Beach: *Judy Watts.* **197** Long Point: *Janet K. Woodcock.* **198** Plum Island: *Kenneth D. Mandl.* **199** Federal house. *Frederica Matera.* **Regional Source Guide: page 200** Signs, Center Sandwich. *Frederica Matera.* **203** Languishing statuary. *Frederica Matera.* **204** Meetinghouse, Center Sandwich. *Frederica Matera.*

Index

Page numbers in *italics* indicate photographs and captions.

About the Authors

Jane Holtz Kay

For almost two decades since her graduation from Radcliffe, Jane Holtz Kay has written on her native city and region as an architecture critic for the *Boston Globe*, the *Nation*, and the *Christian Science Monitor*. Her first book, *Lost Boston*, a history of how the city grew, illustrated by photos of buildings that have been demolished, has become a preservation classic. She is the author of the introduction of Pantheon's *WPA Guide to Massachusetts* and has written articles for such publications as the *New York Times*, *Progressive Architecture*, *Smithsonian*, *Saturday Review*, and *Historic Preservation*.

Pauline Chase-Harrell

Pauline Chase-Harrell is a historian, chairperson of the Boston Landmarks Commission, and partner in Boston Affiliates, a firm specializing in historic exhibitions and interpretations. She is the author of *Arrowhead Farm: Three Hundred Years of New England Husbandry and Cooking*.